A Son of the South Bay:

Part 1: The Early Years

Chris Lawler

ISBN: 9798576235797

This is a memoir from an old and fragmented mind. Most of it is truthful, as far as I can remember. Some of it is fictional, but *plausible*. I had to fabricate certain connecting material to make these stories flow. There are certain characters that show up in these stories that are real people. For others, I have changed their names to protect privacy. The real people who I name are accurately depicted as I remember. The anonymous characters are subject to my liberty with the facts.

I swear no oath as to the accuracy of this memoir. Even my own sisters say I've got things all wrong. Typical. Fine. Let them write their own snoozy memoirs to set me straight. I bet mine is a whole lot more fun to read. In the end, you decide. Make sure you let them know.

To my autistic son James, who made a habit of waking up at 4 AM every morning, dragging me out of bed, and giving me the space and time to write freely.

To my wife Susan, a relentless updraft to my spirit. Always in my corner, sometimes in my face. Her steadfast love is a gift.

To my best friend Gabby, who wove many of these tales with me and who set an example of excellence that was easy for an old furniture repairman to follow.

A Son of the South Bay

2020

Introduction

I don't know why you are reading this. There are way groovier bios of beach people you could spend your time reading. Try 'Gidget'. At least she's cute. I'm just an old man who was once a kid roaming around the Beach Cities in the late sixties and seventies, trying to find my way in life. Writing these stories has been very therapeutic to me. It's been forcing me to rummage through my leathery brain where I threw all these memories and stitch my past back together like a crazy quilt.

I didn't think I was writing a book. This all started when I discovered a large group on Facebook dedicated to remembering the South Bay. 'You probably grew up in Manhattan or Hermosa Beach if....' People were posting old photos and various memories. I got drawn in and hooked. I began sharing little memories about my years in the South Bay, and people liked it. They kept giving me little 'sardine treats' in the comments, and, like a trained seal, I kept writing. Now my IPad is lousy with all these stories. I have heeded the call to put them together in a book. So, this is your fault. None of this would have been possible without my South Bay Facebook family's love. I will always be grateful.

I'm going to continue throwing these bits out there as I write them. That will give you all some equity in this project. By the time it's all done, you will all own a piece of me. Hey, you can show it in your front window like that tramp leg lamp from 'Christmas Story'. It will be a Major Award.

Part 1 - The Pilgrim

The South Bay of Los Angeles

The South Bay is the area south and west of the greater Los Angeles basin. It is bordered on the Westside by the Pacific Ocean; the north, south, and eastern borders are hotly debated. That's because most people want to identify with the South Bay the way the French want to identify with the Riviera. I get it. The South Bay is one of the gems of LA. No one close wants to be left out.

If I were a generous man, I would lay a fuzzy boundary line at LAX for the Northern boundary, run that east about five miles past the 405 Freeway to capture Inglewood, then turn south through Hawthorne, Gardena, and East Torrance. Maybe pick up some of Carson. The border then follows the 110 Freeway south through Wilmington, Lomita, Harbor City, and San Pedro. The Southern boundary is the ocean south of the Palos Verdes Peninsula. The Harbor area and Long Beach are their own entities.

If you are (or were) lucky enough to live in this little slice of the sandbox, you have had a very different experience of Los Angeles than most folks. Outside the sandbox, people think of LA as a smog-choked traffic jam where everyone is trying to get to that audition or take a meeting with producers or shoot up a rival gang's neighborhood before the earthquakes take us all out. People say we have no changes of seasons in Southern California. Of course, we have seasons. We have Summer, Cooler Summer, Wet Summer, and Almost Summer Again. We also have Earthquake Season, Riot Season, and Giant Forest Fire Season. Yes, it's like one big disaster movie being shot by all the movie studios at once. But inside the South Bay sandbox, life is soothed by the music of eternally lapping waves. The smog is pushed past the 405, and Coppertone and sea salt scent the air. When you stand on the shore, the ocean just drains the stress out of your bones. The Pacific kisses your feet with the same primal love that was here at the beginning of time.

Nothing this good stays undiscovered for long. Even the French Riviera was a sleepy little beach town once upon a time. So, of course, the South Bay is crowded. Heck, you can't swing a dead cat without hitting a producer, a pro athlete, or a fossilized swinger on the Strand. The real estate prices have shot to the moon. The flow of traffic down Manhattan Beach Blvd. is glacial at times. And the charming little beach cottages that used to serve as vacation homes for Hollywood executives have mostly been replaced by multistory McMansions. None of that matters to those of us who lived here. Once the sand gets between your toes, it never goes away. I will always be a son of the South Bay.

A Taste of Tiki Apartments and Muzak

I am not a native to the South Bay. I'm an import from the Valley. Now, my parents were South Bay kids all the way. Of course, when they grew up, they found out they couldn't afford to live there as adults and had to move away. Boy, that's an old story. Anyway, they found cheap veteran housing in the North San Fernando Valley and moved there to spawn. The marriage didn't last, and when I was a few months old, my mom kicked my father (Blain) to the curb and hooked up with my step-dad, Jack. That was all a horrible tragedy that I was just too young to get. My older sisters caught some of the drama, but they were only 1 and 2 years older than me, so not much. Back in those days, adults thought that if you got divorced, the best thing would be to get out of the way and let the new family bond. So Blain stood down and stayed out of the picture for a few years. I know he regretted that play because, as a baby boy, Jack was the only dad I knew. I never bonded to Blain as my father; he was just this nice visiting man that brought funny gifts once in a while.

(Word to the wise: Don't give up your first few years with your kids even if the marriage is DOA. If you don't lay the foundation of bonding while they are runts, it won't be there, and you will regret it when you are old and need someone to change your diaper.)

Lake View Terrace, in the northeast corner of the San Fernando Valley, was a little bedroom community that couldn't decide if it was going to be a ghetto or a hideous ghetto. It was a hotbed of racial tension in the mid-sixties. It sat right next to Pacoima, a mostly black neighborhood. That made LVT an easy punching bag for frustrated black rioters during the Civil Rights protests. I knew next to nothing about any of that. All I knew was that after Dr. Martin Luther King was shot, the whole neighborhood got a new script from somewhere up above, and life became dreadful. We had trucks roaming the street, taking potshots at random houses. Everyone was fearful. Bullies tormented me at school, and I had no dad there to tell me what to do. My mom was slipping into alcoholism, and my Bi-Polar grandma moved in. Thank God for TV. I watched TV all day long. Lucas McCain, the Rifleman, basically raised me. Captain Kangaroo was my Grandpa, and Astro-boy was my alter-ego. My mom didn't care. They didn't know about TV obsession back then. I think she was just relieved I had something to occupy my time.

We lived for ten years in Lake View Terrace. My mom was dating her new boyfriend Jack a lot, and finally, Jack married mom, and they popped out my little sister, Syndie, five years younger than me. Jack and Mom began to fight, so one day, Jack left. I cried an ocean of tears, but it didn't matter. He left our family in Lake View Terrace to move into a detached, free-standing, cab-over camper that sat in his Grandmother's driveway in North Redondo. He tried to stay connected. He would drive up to LVT to fight with my mom now and then. Sometimes he would take us all down to his Grandma Fergie's house in North Redondo.

Grandma Fergie lived across the street from an elementary school (now Alta Vista) on Rutland. It was a small house filled with little ceramic chickens, panthers, fancy plates and porcelain statues of black people from the South. That's the way I remember it when I was 5-6 years old. I thought my dad's camper was the coolest hideaway ever. It had a little TV in one cabinet and lots of cowboy stuff my dad liked. Mom and Dad would stay in the camper for some reason while my sisters and I would watch Lawrence Welk and Bonanza with Grandma Fergie until we fell asleep. We would wake up and eat a million pancakes my Grandma Fergie made for us, then go back to the Valley. I didn't really have a concept of where I was; life was just about the house you were in at that time. The idea that the South Bay was different from Lake View Terrace didn't dawn on me until I was a bit older.

Eventually, Jack decided he wasn't coming back to LVT. He had moved out of the camper to an apartment in South Torrance. He hated Lake View Terrace by then, and he wasn't coming back. That left me and my mom and sisters to fend off the injuns on our own. So I lived in this pressurized cauldron of anxiety about getting beat up by bullies, shot or stabbed by rioting black guys, and worrying about my parent's marriage. That's a lot for a kid to think about. So when I got the chance to leave all that behind to visit my step-dad in the South Bay, I did not let the screen door hit me in the butt.

Jack lived in one of those little birdcage apartments built around a pool and decorated with so much tiki swag that it looked like the Big Kahuna exploded there. He shared this pad with a guy I never saw 'cause he was always gone when my dad brought me there. My dad had a TV but didn't let me watch it much. He just told me to get outside and find something to do. Funny world back then, right? Just send your eight-year-old out the door and not even look back. That's the way they rolled in '66.

Getting outside meant going to an empty lot next door with my dad's hammer and pounding ant hills. This was one of my favorite loner things to do that I picked up in the Valley. In LVT, they have giant red ants that sting like they hate you. My revenge was to systematically destroy their ant colony with a hammer while playing out a monster movie in my head. If I was lucky enough to have a magnifying glass, it was even better. Burn, baby, burn! Geeze, that's not psychotic at all.

I only have a vague impression of where this apartment was in the South Bay. I think it was inland, sort of near the 405. I remember seeing a playground with Indian-style Tee-Pee structures as we got near the off-ramp to get to the apt. Maybe someone knows where this was? Anyway, it was like heaven to me. All the tension from the Valley just drained away as we pulled up to the Tiki Apartment Bldg. even the Tiki motif was soothing. A giant tiki statue out front greeted me. It said without words, "Aloha, Bwana. You not in da war zone any longer, little brah. Just relax. Every ting gonna be A'aight."

My dad, (step-dad, actually) was not super affectionate with me, but I think he was trying his best to make 'moments'. He had a big jar of Nestlé's Quick on the kitchen counter and lots of milk, and he said I could have it anytime I wanted. There were cookies there and even a box of See's candy; everything my mom said was bad for me. If all this was bad, tie me to the whipping post. I now wonder if he was taking a shot at my mom by all this indulgence. I pondered that over a huge glass of chocolate milk and a plate of donuts.

On this particular weekend, my dad had a job Saturday installing linoleum in a kitchen in Wilmington. I remember it was Wilmington because the air smelled like oil and all the people were Filipino. My dad was a master at his craft. When he fired up his blowtorch to soften the linoleum, I thought he was a god. I tried to help out cleaning up as he made messes during the installation. A tiny, impossibly wrinkled Filipino grandma thought I was cute and gave me some weird pastry that tasted like sweet frog meat. After one bite of exploration, a second bite out of shock, and a third bite to confirm my horror, I pretended to go to the bathroom so I could flush it away. I stayed away from the frog cookies, or 'croakies', the rest of the day.

At the end of the job, my dad told the lady to be careful not to walk on the new floor with all her weight for the next few hours. It was his favorite joke. Most customers got it and laughed, but a few hopped around on their tippy-toes as they went to get their checkbook. Those were moments we lived for. I just smiled, and my dad would wink at me. So great to be in on a joke and not the object of it. Jack always made me feel I was in and never out. Know what I mean?

After that job, we went to Sambo's for dinner. Remember Sambo's? A restaurant with racially inspired decor that would never be seen in today's PC world. Jack let me order a steak. "Work like a man, eat like a man," was his motto. After we got back to the apartment, we went swimming, watched 'Man from UNCLE' and then got ready for bed.

Jack set me up on the living room sofa and turned on the radio. Maybe he thought I was like a puppy that needed the soothing. I didn't complain. I figured he would put on KHJ or some country

17

station that played the Johnny Cash and Roy Orbison music he
liked. To my surprise, he found a station that played elevator
music. I didn't mind. I hadn't become snobby in my musical
DNA yet. Whatever my Daddy liked, I liked. In fact, I LOVED
IT. It was an FM station that played those soft Muzak style tunes
that the Jackie Gleason Orchestra used to specialize in. They
were rich with shimmering violins and featured Melodicas, those
harmonica sounding instruments that wove soft, optimistic,
sentimental melodies around fluffy comforting orchestrations.
You hardly ever hear that kind of music anymore, but when I do,
it takes me all the way back to '67, falling asleep on my dad's
sofa, safe from the jungle of Lake View Terrace and wondering
if I had a place there, in the South Bay.

Lake View Terrace Breaks Down

Back in the 'hood of Lake View Terrace, things were falling apart. I was getting too old to hide from growing up anymore. Until then, life was mostly watching TV, playing with a few friends on my street, going to school, and dodging bullies. I kept my life small and manageable. I only had three friends, a black kid and a Jewish kid up the street and a feral rat-kid from a few blocks away. The black kid was slowly leaving the innocence of childhood where no one knows they are black, white, or brown. That was a sweet time of pure laughter, Tonka trucks, and sloppy fudgesickles. He began cutting his mooring line because I was getting to be a drag on his new groove. He was becoming a soul brotha, a 'playa', and I was no good to him, not even as a comic relief sidekick. The Jewish guy from the Perfect Family was following his parent's lead as they increasingly hid from my dysfunctional family. We were too awkward to relate to anymore. I agreed, but the option to run away from home and join their perfect kosher tribe was not on the menu. Our functional friendship was expiring. He grew tired of kicking my ass in Monopoly, plus he was getting even more Jewishly the older he got, and I couldn't keep up. He drifted to Hebrew school for friends. That left me with the feral rat-kid.

This freckly, spike hair kid was Nick. He was a flawed, twisted, vaguely dangerous 'oops' child of a swinging couple. His breeding stock was a mystery, and the current alpha male of his house was more inclined to eat him than raise him. This kid found me and hung on for dear life. We clicked in a creepy way. He used to maintain a little cemetery in the corner of his backyard. It had small headstones and homemade crosses. The graves contained the corpses of tiny animals and insects that he found dead (or made dead?). He took a dubious scientific interest in them. He would dig them up from time to time to inspect their state of decay. Nick deliberately set up the graveyard to be as ghoulish as it could be. I became fascinated by his dedication to his craft. In a pre-goth world, he just wanted to be morbidly horrifying. Cool. I took the ride. He was like Dracula, and I was his Renfield. On Saturday afternoon, we watched classic horror movies together and took notes. We always rooted for Godzilla, Frankenstein, the Mummy, Wolfman, or whatever monster was featured on the 'Chiller' TV show. From anyone's outsider viewpoint, we were total sickos. His parents didn't care what he did, and mine never knew. He was my last friend in Lake View Terrace just before we moved, so I couldn't be too picky. At last, the wheels fell off.

Nick had a plan. He asked him to meet for a secret campfire talk in a big drainpipe at 4 am. I drank a bunch of water before I went to bed the night before, so I would have to wake up early. That's an old Indian trick I learned from a western. At 4 am, or so, my bladder dragged me out of bed. My brain was still asleep, so I almost peed in my closet before realizing it wasn't the bathroom. I got to the bathroom just in time. I quietly put on my pants and grabbed my shoes, and snuck out of my house while it was still dark. Everything was so quiet; you could hear the traffic from the Golden State freeway 5 miles away (the 210 wasn't built yet). I crept through the empty streets to the big drain pipe that went under Terra Bella. A faint glow could be seen inside. I slid down the embankment and peeked inside the pipe. There was Nick, with an exciting little fire snapping away. I sat down and fed bits of trash into the fire as he told me his plan. He said he was bored with finding dead birds and cockroaches. He wanted to kill a small animal like a rat or a dog. WTF? Just like that, I was looking for the off-ramp of this friendship. I had no stomach for murder. After that little chat, I avoided him like a bear trap.

Now I was truly a loner. Faith grade was coming to an end at Fenton Ave. Elementary school. One more year, and I would have to survive racially violent McClay Jr. High. This was a terrifying prospect to me. I began to plan my escape. I thought if I could hike from LVT to Redondo Beach, Jack, my step-dad, would surely take me in. It was a desperate move, but I thought I would have a mental breakdown if I stayed. I didn't know who I was supposed to be, what I was supposed to do, or where I was supposed to belong. I just knew it was NOT going to be in Lake View Terrace.

Fortunately, other forces were at work to move me along. My mom and dad were trying to reboot their marriage. I guess Jack had decided he was not going to move back to LVT. He had floor covering work in the South Bay, so the only option was to sell the house and move there with him. Everyone in my family was happy with this decision. We all started to prepare. We weren't just moving to a new address; we were moving to a new state of mind.

Big Apartments and Little Pink Pills

I was about nine years old when my mom decided to move us to Torrance in the South Bay, where my dad lived. The war between my parents had cooled, so they decided to make a new start of it. Thank God. They had no idea of what a nervous wreck I was becoming.

By that time, I had no friends left, and the bullies in my LVT neighborhood were drunk on the fear that I generated. They were a constant threat every time I went outside. My life had shrunk down to just a few spots of isolation where I could play and get through a day in relative safety. Looking back now, I think there was little danger, but when fear gets into a small boy's head, it changes the color of everything he sees. It also makes him eat.

I was getting fat from eating to compensate and sitting around all day watching TV. My step-dad began to lose interest in me and judge me for the cream puff I was becoming. My mom began to worry. She knew what to do. She took me to her 'Diet Doctor'.

Mom was on a first-name basis with her Diet Doctor. He was very important to her. Especially now, when the prospect of the Beach life was just around the corner. She was hell-bent on getting in competitive shape so she could hold her own against the bikini girls of Hermosa. The Diet Doctor gave her ammunition in the form of these tiny pink pills. I don't know what they were, but in 1966, many things were available that you can't get now unless you 'know a guy. 'Mom had been taking these pills for a while, so why wouldn't she think it was a good idea to help her chubby son in the same way? The Diet Doctor gave me my own prescription. I took my first pill the next morning before school.

Oh..My..God. School became the most interesting, fascinating, amazing thing I could possibly do. I mean everything about it; the desks, the books, the shape of the clock on the wall, the teacher's horn-rimmed glasses, the lunch bag, and even the edges of the No. 9 pencil in my hand became endlessly fascinating. It was no trouble at all paying attention to my teacher's lectures. Every delicious word that fell from her lips splashed in my mind with a sparkling cascade of delightful importance. The entire world became high definition, Technicolor spectacular. It wasn't hallucinogenic; I didn't see psychedelic visions, but I had the stamina of an oak tree, the energy of a tornado, and the vision of an eagle. The darkness of fear had been banished. Television became a total waste of time that I could spend exploring the Land of Oz around me. Are you getting the picture? I never knew what these little pink pills were, but I couldn't wait for the next day to take another one.

The 'diet 'worked. In the couple of months before we moved, I lost 15-20 pounds, I think. When the Diet Doctor saw the results, he considered the goal achieved and cut off the prescription. We moved to West Torrance that week. We set up in a three-bedroom unit in the Bay Village Apartment complex on Anza, and I was lost. Fear closed back in. The world became black and white again. I didn't know who the bad guys were, so I assumed everyone was a threat. I had no desire to explore my new world, no desire to leave the apartment. TV and eating reacquainted themselves. And then one day, I discovered my little pink friends again.

My parents had their own bathroom connected to their bedroom. This bathroom was supposed to be off-limits, but sometimes the main bathroom was occupied, and when you gotta go, you gotta go. I went in there to use it, and it was a wreck with lady junk all over and a countertop filled with hair and makeup products. Then I saw it. A tiny pink pill sitting by itself in the corner that seemed to say, "Hey, big boy, where you been?"

It had been a few weeks since my prescription ran out. At the sight of this little pill, a sickening pulse of hope burped out. Could this be my leetle compares that I spent so many fiestas with? It had no markings. It could have been a contraceptive pill for all I knew. But I didn't think so. I took that little pill and waited to see what would happen.

In ten minutes, I felt my vision sharpen. In fifteen minutes, the avocado green kitchen table became fascinating. In a half-hour, the whole Mardi Gras was loose in my head. I was rolling down Bourbon Street in a ticker-tape parade to welcome me home.

I stepped out of the apartment fearless. I walked to the central lobby past a wad of teenagers and didn't even give them a glance. Out the door on Anza, then south to Torrance Blvd and west to where I knew the ocean was. Every step along the way was supercharged with interest. Past the Daily Breeze building, past the crest of the hill at Prospect, down to Veterans Park, and out onto the horseshoe pier at Redondo. It took no time at all. I wasn't running, but my engine was burning rocket fuel, and my feet ate the ground. On the Pier, there was such a sensory overload I just slowed my steps to a crawl and opened my mind wide like a whale shark to take in the krill. I remember a song by America was playing on the PA, 'A horse with No Name. 'I actually understood it! I ended up down at the lower level fish market exploring fish faces

Then I started re-entering the atmosphere. Pinky was wearing off, and I'm a long way from home. I started back, but before I got to prospect, I was pretty much on my own. By the time I passed The Daily Breeze building, I was flat lining and taking on fear like a torpedoed ship. I felt like every eye in the world was watching me; every bad guy in every ally was stalking me. It was terrifying. By the time I got to the T.G. &Y. On Anza, I was dying of thirst. I hadn't been drinking any water the whole time. I bought a Coke and guzzled it down. That got me back to Bay Village. I crawled back to my apartment. My mom was cooking dinner. She was happy that I had finally got outside 'to make some friends. 'She had no clue. After dinner, I went straight to bed and slept for a month (it seemed).

The next day, I had to go to the bathroom and wouldn't you know it? Someone was in the main bathroom just then. I had been waiting for hours for this 'funny coincidence 'to line up. So, gosh darn it, I was FORCED to go to Mom's bathroom. Once in, with the door locked, I looked very closely at the mess she kept in there. Nothing on the counter. Nothing in the drawers. I looked in the cabinet behind the mirror. Nothing, nothing... Wait... Ahh, Bingo! There it is. A little bottle tucked away back, half-filled with little pink compadres. I took out three. She would never miss them.

The next few days were equally outstanding in the South Bay. I became a fearless nine-year-old. As long as the pinks held me up, I could do anything. Then they ran out, and I revisited the bathroom. The location of the bottle had changed. It wasn't up high in the mirror cabinet; now, it was down deep in the back of a lower cabinet. It took me fifteen minutes to find them. Hmm... What could this mean? Did she notice the missing pills? Was she on to me? I stole another three pills so I could ponder the problem with clarity.

A few days later, I made sure my mom was gone, and I went looking for more, but they were nowhere to be found. I looked for a half hour. When I realized that I was not going to find them, panic set in. I sat on the toilet seat and had a breakdown moment that changed my life.

Terror seemed to fill that bathroom from the bottom to the top. I knew life couldn't go on taking pills, but I also felt I couldn't live without them, that I didn't WANT to live without them. It's an addict's bind. I knew I was in the grip of these pills. I broke down crying and said out loud, "GOD HELP ME." I kept praying like that through my blubbering. I had never prayed out of desperation before, so I didn't know how to do it right. I just kept saying out loud, "God, please help me. I'm in trouble. Please help me!"

Just then, my older sister opened the door. "What are you doing?" she asked. Adrenaline shot up my spine. I had been lost in the moment and had no idea how loud I was getting. I stumbled over my answer. "I, I, I'm practicing a song, yeah, a song I wrote!" Her eyes went to slits and her tumblers were rolling. I don't think she bought my story, but I didn't wait around to discuss it. I bolted out of there and out of the apartment and went into the field behind. I sat on a lump of dirt clods and waited for my adrenaline to settle down.

Two things happened. First, my lust for these pills snapped off clean that instant. I had no desire to get to that Mardi Gras or even look for the pills anymore. I never saw one again. Secondly, I knew God had heard me and helped me. He stopped this addiction in its tracks. His act wasn't spooky or mystical, but it wasn't a casual flip of a nickel to a beggar. God had come in that bathroom and bent the rules of physics. It was a 'shock and awe 'moment when you stand too close as a train rushes by. God saved me from replicating my mom's addiction and put Himself right there on the dashboard of my life. I didn't become a church-going Christian or even religious; I just knew there was something bigger than me out there, and it (He) saved me.

~~~

Looking back, I now realize that my mom was a full-blown addict/alcoholic by that time. She still kept up a reasonable front, but she was breaking. If you have read me much, you know I'm pretty tough on my mom. I hardly ever mention her unless it's to say she was an addict. That's because I have a lot of anger about what was lost. The sweet mommy I knew as a child was systematically butchered by addiction. Parts of who she was disappeared every day. What filled the space left behind was a ravenous monster desperate for the next fix or drink. By the time I was in my early teens, she was just a hollowed-out shell. Her original personality (that I faintly remembered) was gone and never came back.

She had a pivotal moment when I was 13 when she gave up alcohol cold turkey. I didn't see it then, but the courage it took to do this without the help of rehab or AA was her most heroic moment. Still, the years of use left her with the mental maturity of a twelve-year-old. She became desperately insecure and leaned on me (as the only man in her life) for all her validation. I admit this was not a burden I was willing or prepared to carry. I failed her there because I was utterly outgunned and full of my own drama. I wish I had a do-over there.

The alcohol was gone, but the prescription drugs continued. Mom had seven different doctors prescribing her drugs. She used a different alias for each one. Years after I moved away and was busy building my own family, she moved closer to my little sister's family in Fresno and became a beloved 'Nana 'to her kids. Seems she grew a new, replacement personality. I'm glad for that; for her. I'm sad that I can't remember much about her without the addiction polluting the vision. She passed away in her mid-fifties. Someday, beyond the end of this life, I will see her again without the damage. She put the kernel of faith in me when I was little. She was the reason I knew to call upon God for rescue. For that, I will be eternally grateful.

I'm thinking about some of you reading this that might be in that addict's bind. I wish I could say that I could call out to God for you and snap that thing off clean. If it were that easy, I would have done it for some of my own family. Don't think I haven't tried. Maybe you have to call out for yourself? I don't know. Sometimes God sends help to lead you out of the jungle, and occasionally he sends a helicopter to pull you out. It's His prerogative. I got yanked out of trouble. No matter how rescue comes, I believe it can happen for you; then, you will write a story like this of your own. Peace.

Dumb Farmhand

After my brush with addiction, I had to start dealing with life at a regular speed. I went out the door and outback behind my building. There were usually a bunch of kids out there at all times of the day. On one particular day, a sound caught my attention. A Siren song, irresistible to boys, filled the air. It was coming from the far side of the field, where a dirt road ran along a fenced-off drainage sump. A bunch of boys clustered out there, taking turns riding a minibike.

Nowadays, there are all kinds of dirt bikes, pocket rockets, trikes, quads, and everything in between for kids that need speed. Back then, everything that burned gas was for adults, except these homemade, lawnmower engine powered, tube framed mini bikes. I was sucked in by the sound of that popping, sputtering two-stroke engine, so I crossed the field and joined the rabble.

The owner of this magical machine was a Mexican kid about my age. Juan was cool. He was clearly basking in the glory of his minibike, and he was using it to make instant paper-mâché friends with every kid in earshot. He was letting anyone who showed up take a ride down the dirt road and back. Juan took every third or fourth ride for himself, but no one complained.

Soon he turned to me and said, "It's your turn, man. Go ahead." I straddled the bike and sat down on the warm seat, a little unsure how to do it. I didn't want to ask for help for fear that I would lose my turn. I just torqued the right handle, and the mini bike surged forward. I torqued it a little further, and it jumped out down the road. Exhilarating! I opened the bike up as far as it would go. It had a speed governor to hold it to an easy cruise, but it was fast enough to make hanging onto the bumpy dirt road a challenge. 'Prapp-pa-pa-pa-pa... Pop-pop-pop-pop... Praaaaap-pap-pap'. I never had so much fun squeezed into 45 seconds in my life.

When the mini bike ran out of gas, the fans melted away. I helped Juan push the bike back to his house, which was right next to my apartment building on Anza. Juan lived with his father in a little house with a small farm in the back. It was the only property like it on the street, a hold out from development. I heard about people who refused to sell out to developers, but I thought that only happened in New York. The land that went with the little house was big and deep. It could easily be another big apartment building. Eventually, it would be.

Mr. Alvarez (?) had no wife but clearly loved his only son. I think he knew that his boy had a few stigmas to overcome. Juan stuck out because he was Apache-Mexican, fairly poor, and everyone knew he was a farmer boy. It seems ridiculous by today's standard, but there weren't a lot of Mexicans living in that area back then. Few black people either, or Asians or any other race for that matter. The blending of all the races hadn't happened yet in that part of the South Bay. It was a 'Leave it to Beaver' neighborhood stuffed with white bread. So Mr. Alvarez tried to give his son whatever advantage he could. The mini bike overcame a lot of stigmas, but only for as long as the gas held out. I was the only kid who came home with Juan.

As soon as Juan put the bike away, he had to do chores. When you live on a farm, the chores never stop. I had nothing to do and nowhere to go, so I helped. We raked up weeds, fed the chickens in a little coop, and collected eggs. It was cool. The relationship Juan had with his dad reminded me of the Rifleman TV show.

I was at their little farmhouse once when Mr. Alvarez asked me in Spanish if I wanted to make some money. Juan translated. He asked me to pull weeds from his extensive vegetable garden. I agreed because I wanted the money, and it felt like I was in an episode from the Rifleman. So, he showed me where to work and left me to it while he took his son to a doctor's appointment or something.

When he came back a few hours later, he and Juan walked out back with me so I could show off my work. I had cleared a huge piece of land. The dirt was raked neatly, and everything green was piled up at the compost pile. Not bad, huh? They looked at each other and rattled off a bunch of Spanish that didn't sound too good. Mr. Alvarez went back into the house. Juan stayed behind to explain. I had pulled up the weeds but also the entire crop of cilantro and onions. I thought they were all weeds. How would a stupid city slicker kid know? I was so embarrassed. Mr. Alvarez came back out with some money and paid me. He was disappointed but not mad. There was forgiveness in his sun-baked eyes. He knew I was just an ignorant gringo, but he appreciated the hard work I had put in. He put his leathery hand on my head, said something in Spanish, and mussed my hair, and even laughed a little. The next day, Juan and I replanted the area I cleared.

In the six weeks I knew them; I got so bonded that it tore my heart when Mr. Alvarez sold out and moved away. (Maybe he couldn't make his mortgage because he lost his onion crop?) I never saw them again, and a new apartment building went up right away.

This episode from my life reminds me that even with the best intentions, I sometimes pull up the crop instead of the weeds. Now I'm a Dad and a church elder and a business owner and boss to my employees. I've got a lot of responsibility. But what if I'm still an ignorant farmhand? Will the people around me survive my good intentions? God can probably out-produce my mistakes. Please forgive me if I'm reaching for your stalk. I mean well, but sometimes it's all just greens to me.

Bare Foot'n

When I first moved to the South Bay from Lake View Terrace in the San Fernando Valley, I thought I was a tough kid. I was used to hiking around the Hansen Dam wilderness area all day when I was ten. Most of that hiking was barefoot. Heck, shoes almost never touched our feet all summer long out there. The Valley is a furnace in the summer, but we would walk on the hot asphalt, through the fields, sticker bushes, and gravel without a second thought.

I had tough, leathery 'Indian feet', my Indian Granny used to say. She said it was a gift from the Cherokee Tribe. I'm only like 1/64th Cherokee Indian, but I've learned to make a big deal out of it. I assume all you white Devils wouldn't understand, but my Native Brothers and I think nothing of going barefoot anywhere. It makes it easier to sneak up on a mountain lion (as if).

So, when Mom offered to drop me off at the beach for the day, I didn't think about shoes at all. I would walk home to Anza Ave (near West High School) at the end of the day, no problem.

Mom dropped me off at Pier Ave in Hermosa Beach about 10 am on a beautiful summer Sunday. I walked a few blocks south and turned into the sand around 10th Street. I threw my towel down just short of the wet sand and stood there taking it in. The sun was warm and laughed over small puffy clouds that moseyed like a herd of sheep. The Beach Boys came drifting over the sand from some house on the Strand. The smell of Coppertone, mixed with the aroma from someone's barbecue, filled the air with the holy incense of beach worship. I walked out into the water as clear as a glass-bottom boat. The little shore fish dodged and played around my knees. How can this get any better?

The surf was great. I tried hard to body surf like I saw other guys doing, but I didn't really know how. Didn't matter. Out there in the water with me were girls wearing bikinis so small they looked like pirates' eye patches. I stayed in the water all day until about 4 pm. Then I grabbed my towel and headed home. What I didn't count on was my feet soaking in ocean brine all day, scuffing the sandy bottom for hours and returning to infant like tenderness. All my tough Indian callouses were gone. The bottom of my feet were soft as a baby's cheek. After walking one block, I knew I was in trouble.

All my Cherokee ancestors watched from the Great Hunting Ground in the Sky, laughing at this poor white boy. I only had enough Cherokee blood to fill a thimble, but I had enough Cherokee pride to fill the ocean. This was the beginning of the Ordeal. I had to hike that six miles back to Torrance on my baby-soft bare feet, or everything I believed about myself was a lie. I sang my death-song and began.

So me and my baby feet were in trouble. I walked south down the Hermosa Strand as far as it went and turned inland at Herondo, which becomes Anita that turns into 190th when it goes over the hill. The Strand is white concrete, but when you make that turn inland, there is a lot of black asphalt in your path.

I looked for grass at every step along the way, but there are not many lawns in that neighborhood. Those painted white road stripes became my best friend. Not just because they were cooler, but they were smooth. Sadly, you only get them when you're crossing a road. By the time I crested the hill at 190th, I was in such agony that even if I were able to walk across the backs of naked virgins all the way home, it wouldn't have mattered. Still, I paused and smiled at the thought. If you could find enough virgins in the whole South Bay to make a path, they would all be ten-year-old dorky boys like me. Not sure why they had to be naked, though. I digress...

I had to get to a neighborhood where there was grass. I turned south at Prospect and then east at Beryl Street and dove into a residential area unknown to me. I figured if I kept going east, at some point, I would hit Anza. Well, I found the grass I was looking for, but I also found dogs. It seemed like every house had a dog who was angry that I was alive. They hated that I walked on their grass. What if people were like that? What if every time I passed a house, a housewife or an old man came to the screen door and cussed me out at the top of their lungs? My mind kept seizing ideas like this to keep from thinking about pain. It worked. I got to Anza and Del Amo with about a quarter-mile to go.

By this time, my feet were bleeding some. Even the grass was painful. I had to do something. I found a liquor store that had boxes in the back. I tore some cardboard off and put it in the bottom of some plastic bags. I tied these on my ankles, and what a relief! I'm sure it didn't look so good, but it got me all the way back to the Bay Village apartments. My feet were throbbing like war drums, but I didn't say anything to my mom. I got a tube of

Oro-jell, the teething medicine, and rubbed it on my sore dogs. It numbed them for a while

My Ordeal was over. The thunder of laughter coming from the Great Hunting Ground in the Sky was silenced by 'Dragging Canoe,' the Chickamauga Warrior Clan's Chief. He changed my Cherokee name from 'Rain Cloud' (because I was always crying as a kid) to 'Hop Footing Water Logged Squaw Squealer'. I go with 'Hop Foot' for short. My Cherokee ancestors were pleased. From time to time, I commemorate my crucible by dressing up my thumb (1/64 of me) in ceremonial war paint and doing an Indian dance to frighten the rest of the white Devils in my own family.

Gabby and Me

My family was thoroughly installed in the family apartment complex, Bay Village, and life had changed radically. I went from living in my own house with a big front and back yard to living with neighbors, one thin wall away on each side. The apartment was styled after the late '60's mod influences. It had avocado green kitchen counters and low shag carpeting. When my Mom added our Mid-century refugee furniture, the place came alive with a groove Austin Powers could understand.

We had an upstairs apartment with a long staircase that fell to the front door below. That stairwell would become quite a hangout for my two older sister's pre-teeny girlfriends. They would clog up the exit, so I had to climb over them to get to the door below. If that meant I had to touch and rub up against them as I squeezed by, well, it couldn't be helped.

Bay Village was massive. It occupied half a block of the street front on Anza and had nine wings of apartments (up and downstairs) stretching out behind. Carports under all. It was a whole universe in itself, in my eleven-year-old mind. I was still a loner, but as soon as I opened the front door, the shore break of apartment kids was splashing me. It was easy enough to just let go and drift with the tide. I became one of the nameless rabble that roamed aimlessly through the complex.

Kids naturally sort themselves by ages. I hardly ever saw my older sister's gang (except in the stairwell), and my little sister Syndie's herd of tots were invisible to me. Somehow, a narrowly defined 11- 12 year-old rat pack recruited me. At the core of this hive was a queen bee, a girl with so much charismatic magnetism she commanded a tribe of her own. I'll call her Tracy (not her real name), and I fell under her spell along with twenty-odd other boys and girls who dreamed of getting close to her.

Tracy was on her way to becoming a man killer. She had hypnotic hips, long blond hair, and a relatively flat-chested front she liked to reveal with open buttoned blouses that were as seductive as they were innocent. Yet, it was the spark in her eye that made it all work. She was quick with an inclusive smile and a sideways look that made you feel like you were her favorite. Strong Mojo. I had no chance.

I fell in with her tribe and attended to her in her empty apartment while her parents were at work. We really didn't do anything, just hung around, but you felt as if something special, maybe naughty, was about to happen. It was in this platoon of boy slaves that I discovered Gabby.

More like he discovered me. He was a skinny kid with ears that stuck who wore a devilish grin on his face at all times. We gravitated to each other because of our Three Stooges' sense of humor. When I made some snarky remark in the middle of Linda's gang, he was the one who laughed. If I were working up a prank, he always wanted in on it. He had some of the best ideas for goofing off and disrupting the order of the gang. We just thought we were hilarious, even if everyone else thought we were punks. It didn't take long to realize that it was Gabby that I was looking for when I reported for duty every day.

He was under Tracy's spell like everyone else, but, like me, he was just a little too goofy looking to have any real chance with her. There were other, slightly older guys that held her eye. If this gang were a Pirate ship, Tracy would be Captain, the (slightly) older guys were Mates, and Gabby and I were just nameless swabbies on deck. We sometimes became bored and would begin to goof off with each other until Captain Linda's seductive smirk would jerk us back in line. This all changed on Smoking Day.

The property right next to Bay Village was where my first friend, 'Minibike' Juan the Mexican, and his father, Señor Alvarez, had their little farm. They had sold out and moved away, and a new apartment building was being constructed there. It was all scaffolding, bare framing, and construction junk during the day, but it became a playground for a million kids at night when the crews were gone. We used to have crazy games of tag that ranged all over the worksite. We were running over two by fours, swinging from scaffolding and jumping to different levels long before Parkour became a thing. Tracy led us into the construction site as the sun was going down, but it wasn't for tag. We were going to Smoke a Cigarette.

We obediently followed her down into the cinderblock carports. Huddled there in the dark, she struck a match and lit a cigarette. The familiar incense of Mom and Grandma filled the room. She smoked the Marlboro with the ease of a truck stop waitress and passed out cigarettes to the whole gang. There too many of us, so Gabby and I had to share one. We lit it. Gabby tried it, coughed,

41

then passed it to me. I took a drag and wondered what the big deal was. Linda didn't even see us do it. She and her 'officers' were smoking with relish like it was better than ice cream. Huh? It's just a roll of burning leaves with a minty aftertaste. What are we doing this for? Do we think we are going to get laid? Really? Right then, Gabby and I looked at each other and decided to jump ship. We never looked back.

Once detached from that fiefdom, we found that we had a lot in common. We discovered that we lived two doors down from each other. We had neighboring balconies that were separated by an olive tree. This became the scene of ferocious olive wars. We were both from broken homes, both had older and younger sisters, and both had developed a resilient sense of humor that help us survive the drama. We found a partnership where we could do business with each other. Monkey business. Pranks, gags, and tiny froggies were the medium we worked with. We emboldened each other in ways that made life exciting and disgusting. Yet, everything we did was above board: no drugs, pot, or criminal activity. Just modern-day Moe, Larry, and Curly with a dash of Huck and Tom thrown in.

It's hard to relate how important this friend was to me. I have never been easy with making connections. I think God put this goofy kid in my life to save me from being swallowed by a real gang or becoming the first Unabomber. Gabby was easy to be with and had many friends in the complex, but he hung mostly with me for some reason. We ran together all through my time at Bay Village, and even when we both moved away, we worked hard to get together. We didn't go to high school together or even live in the same beach town. Still, we kept the friendship going through the teen years and beyond. That era ended with a momentous hitchhiking trip across the USA and half of Europe. Someday I'll write about that trip. It was once in a lifetime for me but just one of several worldwide expeditions for Gabby.

I humbly admit I needed him more than he needed me. Most of my best memories in this book happened because he was there. Now we are old men and quite different in our outlook on life. He's liberal; I'm conservative. He's secular; I'm a Christian. He has lived all over the US; I've lived in the same house for 40 years. Still, there is no other man dearer to my heart than that goofy kid I met at Bay Village. I hope you get to know and appreciate him the way I do through these memories. I hope there is someone that holds the other end of the story of your life, like my friend Gabby.

Summer School and Froggy Town

At the end of my first year at Grace Wright, I crapped out. I don't know, maybe too much stress at home or just plain laziness put me at the bottom of the class. My mom signed me up for summer school. This would have been a disaster, except that Gabby joined me as an academic bottom feeder. So we both dragged our sorry butts up to Grace Wright on a hot summer day like Tom Sawyer and Huck Finn.

Summer school wasn't like regular school. The teacher knew she was working with hammerheads with no attention span. She did her very best to make the experience fun and educational. Sadly, all she did was set the stage for the Lawler and Hayes Loony Circus.

Our sweet teacher tried to teach us about the real world by setting up an in-class enterprise zone. She assigned different us jobs that earned class script to be spent on goods and services provided by other kids in 'stores.' In this way, we would all learn that hard work and consistent effort would pay off just like in the 'real world.' Stop laughing.

Gabby and I were chosen to run the 'bank.' Big mistake. The first day we were installed in this critical job, we immediately began to turn it into a criminal organization. We stole class script, extorted from other kids, shorted suckers on their pay, and generally became the in-class Mafia. We made such a mess of this sweet teacher's creative plan she had to abandon it and drop into basic math and English gear. We stole her will to live and probably shorten her career by a decade.

The happiest day for her was the day Gabby and I decided to ditch summer school altogether. We still met up every day to 'go to school,' but we never darkened the door at Grace Wright again that summer. Instead, we went to Froggy Town.

Out behind our apartment building, on the far side of the big field where we had dirt clod fights, there was some kind of drainage pit with standing water at the bottom. This big pit was locked behind a chain-link fence to keep knuckleheads like Gabby and me from drowning ourselves in it. Of course, this made it irresistible. So, instead of heading up the Grace Wright to torture the teacher, we jumped the fence and played in the pit.

This pit was absolutely crammed with frogs. At night, the croaking was deafening. During the daytime, there were so many little froggy offspring to play with, we thought we had died and gone to heaven. I'm pretty sure the frogs felt differently.

Now, I'm not going to tell you everything that happened there because there might be young children reading. After all, someday, Gabby or I might be nominated to the Supreme Court. I do not want to have to explain the actions of an eleven-year-old, alone with frogs, to the Senate.

Here are some of the more pleasant highlights.

Froggy Diving Bell

We put a little Froggy in a ball of foil tied to a rock and threw it in the water. We pulled it out and was amazed that the little green Jacques Cousteau had explored the depths and returned to croak the tale.

Froggy Astronaut

Same ball of foil, same frog inside, this time thrown up in the sky as far as we could. Sometimes a water landing, sometimes a land landing, but always a frog happy to get out of the 'spacecraft' alive.

Froggy Voyager

We each made little 'sailboats' out of bits of wood with sticks pushed through paper trash for sails. We tried to get these to sail around, but it got boring until we tied a frog on each one. Then it was Vasco Da Gama vs. Christopher Columbus for domination of the seas.

Froggy Shotgun Wedding

We tied two frogs together in marital bliss with twine and sent them off on their honeymoon. We waited to see how long it would take for them to get 'divorced.'

Froggy Exchange

Basically, we just threw frogs at each other.

Eventually, the summer school session ended, and we were free to give up the pretense. We still went to Froggy Town now and then, but it was never the same. It turns out; it was the ditching that made the pit exciting. Without the ditching, being in the pit just made you a big frog—a big frog with regrets.

~Postscript ~

Dear Froggys,

I want to apologize for disrespecting your right to exist on this planet, in that pit, in peaceful slimy water. I regret the scientific research we performed on your people. Sadly, the only thing we learned was that the most terrifying thing on earth is two eleven-year-old boys with too much time on their hands. These were not my proudest memories. From now on, when one of you looks at me with that wide, sad, Mona Lisa smile, I will pound my heart and bow my head for the Froggy martyrs who taught me to be a better man. I will not dine on your legs. I will not disturb your songs of love and longing in the swamps. I will honor the warts you have given me to remind me to live and let live. Peace. Croak. Or, whatever.

Crabs of King Harbor

Summer in the South Bay in the late sixties was as rich as it was endless. That's what it seemed to me when I was eleven years old. When school let out for the summer, Pandora's Box sprang open full of delightful possibilities. That handful of years around eleven was just the best. I was old enough to range for twenty miles or more without supervision. I had a couple of bucks in my pocket from recycled soda bottles, a sturdy Stingray bike between my legs, and a crazy wingman on my left, my best friend, Gabby. (He always thought I was HIS wingman, poor confused kid).

King Harbor in Redondo was our playground. We would ride there from our apartment building on Anza, west down Torrance Blvd, until we ran out of road. King Harbor was a magic mix of funky bars, smelly boats, tar soaked pier, and just enough wave action to body surf your face into the sand. Inside the 'horseshoe' there were pretty girls in bikinis and oily grandmothers watching their sea monkeys play in the sand. Behind the horseshoe was the inner harbor basin where hoary old fishing boats rocked gently in waters so clear that, when the afternoon light was just right, the whole bottom lit up to show off the octopuses' garden that Ringo sang about.

Gabby and I would sneak into the swarthy bar (don't remember the name) that occupied the lower level of the west side of the inner Basin. It was stuffed with weird junk hanging all over the ceiling and walls—parts of planes, boats, mannequins, fish, concert memorabilia made for a boy's fantasyland. The door was wide open. We would sneak in and rob peanuts from the bar like seagulls snatching fries off the pier.

Just north of the horseshoe at the end of the inner harbor was a small spur of breakwater formed by huge boulders that extended out a little way. Gabby and I loved this rat maze of caves and chambers formed inside the boulders. We loved crawling and spelunking through looking for pirates' treasure. We found no doubloons, but we struck it rich when we realized the treasures of the sea were right there for the taking in the form of thousands of lazy crabs. It was King Neptune's Feast just waiting for us to bring home to our grateful parents. We didn't need crab pots to catch this bounty. We stabbed them with cutlasses (butter knives) and pulled them off into a big plastic trash bag we found. When we had collected about thirty dead crabs, we tied off the bag and headed for home. It only took about two hours in the hot sun to get back (stopping at TG&Y to play ditch and set off all the alarm clocks at once) to Bay Village apartments. We wanted to surprise our families, so we hid the bag by the carports.

After a shower and a few hours watching the Outer Limits and the Three Stooges, everyone got home, and Mom started to work in the kitchen. We snuck out and grabbed the bag (even though something seemed off) and hurried back. "Don't worry about dinner tonight, Mom," I proclaimed. "I have returned from the Sea with a bounty!" I triumphantly ripped open the bag and spilled the 'deadliest catch' on the kitchen floor. Rather than squeals of delight and proud slaps on our backs, my mom screamed. Then it caught up to me. The SMELL. It was horrific! Like the piss of a thousand dead donkeys. The juices oozed out of the putrefying Sea Spiders all over the floor and soaked the edge of our avocado green carpet. I doubled over gagging, and Gabby ran for the hills. CLEAN IT UP BEFORE YOUR DAD GETS HOME was the command my mom gave us. With a clothespin on my nose, we picked up the dead crabs and put them back in the bag, then into another plastic garbage bag and tied it off. We mopped up the crab gravy as best we could. There wasn't enough baking soda in the world to absorb that smell, but we used all we had. When my dad got home, he barely got in the door before he asked, "What the hell died in here?" Mom fingered me. I confessed. He didn't get mad. He loved my spirit of entrepreneurship. Everyone else in my family resented me until we finally went nose-blind to the lingering smell.

I didn't touch a crab for the rest of my life until I visited my new wife's family in Baltimore. Then, when a bushel of steamed Blue crabs was spilled out on the family dinner table, and everyone ripped into them, it all came back. I learned to love it and even make a version of Snow crabs, Baltimore style. That is the penultimate feast for my family today.

The Phantom or Grace Wright

Just north of King Harbor, there was an enclosed, man-made beach with a seawater pool called the Seaside Lagoon. This was a place parents could pay to lay out on the sand and bake while their little kids splashed in the water without the threat of waves. Parents didn't go in the water because it was probably half kid pee. I think there was a bar to serve drinks, lots of umbrellas and beach chairs, and piped in music. I have to reconstruct this scene from second-hand reports because I have no first-hand memory of it even though I went there for a day as an eleven-year-old with Gabby.

Something happened to me there that knocked three days of memory out of my head. I'm told that Gabby and I were goofing off in the sand, and I was running as fast as I could while watching him. I ran right into a stationary lifeguard perch. The lifeguard said I looked like a torpedo coming in full steam. He yelled at me, but I wasn't listening. I impacted the stand on one of the steps that caught my face just under my left eye. Bang! Lights out!

The ambulance was called, and I went to the hospital and had stitches to close the cut. I had a concussion. My face swelled up and turned a kaleidoscope of colors like a Mardi Gras mask. Consciousness came back online a few days later. My memory was wiped blank for three days surrounding the incident, so I have no first-hand recall of the accident. The doctor said I was lucky I didn't lose my eye. Still, the trauma was pretty bad. A huge calcium deposit formed under my eye, and the swollen skin was deep purple, green, yellow, and red. My left eye was completely bloodshot red. I was hideous. The doctor said I had to wear sunglasses to protect my retina from sunlight.

The next Monday, I had to go back to school at Grace Wright Elementary with Gabby. I took the doctor's advice and wore Ray Bans. I added a nice touch to the ensemble by adding a pullover ski mask. I pulled it over my whole head and closed the eye-opening to a narrow slit over the sunglasses. I looked like Gort, the robot from 'The Day the Earth Stood Still.' The other kids loved it. While I was in class, I kept the ski mask rolled up on my head like Mike Nesmith of the Monkees, but it came down at recess, and I was Gort again.

This act went on for some time before I caught the eye of the recess monitor, a tough lady teacher who had a no-nonsense attitude about 6th graders. She came up from behind me, intending to put an end to my showboating on the playground. She yanked the mask off my head along with the sunglasses. I slowly turned around and snarled like the Phantom of the Opera in all my hideous gore. She screamed. She fell over herself to repair my 'medically prescribed' attire, and from that moment on, I owned her. I could have taken her down for being so insensitive to a wounded child. But I remembered. "Klatuu barada nickto."

Carports

The Bay Village apartment complex was infested with kids, like rats on a barge. We were all over every nook and cranny of the building, from the party room to the pool to every little service room and storage locker. It was only a matter of time before we discovered the empty carport lockers.

They were pretty big, about 5 feet tall and 6 feet deep, as I remember. Each apartment had one with assigned parking. Gabby and I found one that belonged to an unoccupied unit. It was unlocked. We moved in and made it our hideout. Over the next few days, we furnished it with a small lamp, a radio, pillows, candles, and other stuff. It was when we found a discarded Playboy magazine that the hideout became the swank lair of the Puberty Brothers.

We had the Porno Palace to ourselves for about a week or so, and we were getting pretty comfortable hanging out in it. If only we could get real girls to join us! How were we supposed to know that this kind of set up would make a normal girl's skin crawl? Worse yet, would we really want to be trapped in this cage with a girl that liked that kind of setup? That's too much thinking for two eleven-year-olds. Thankfully, our plan never had a chance to ripen (or rot).

Gabby and I were up in our swinging bachelor pad one afternoon when the apartment manager came by to show a prospective tenant the carport lockers. We turned off the light and radio and ran 'silent', like a WWII submarine. The tension was building as they got closer and closer. We were inside, so we could not tell if they were talking about our locker or another nearby one.

Their voices grew louder, like depth charges going off closer and closer...
I could feel the panic rise in me... Sweat trickled down my nose, and a drop fell and splashed the floor with a cymbal crash... I bit my lip and looked at Gabby. He just gestured with his hands for me to be calm, cool, and collected. I suddenly had to pee... My leg was getting a cramp... the voices got closer... For heaven's sake, how much strain can a man take? I broke. I threw open the locker door and climbed out, saying something like this:

"Man, you would not believe what is in there! That whole locker is full of dirty pictures! Some pervert probably set the whole thing up!"

The adults were not looking at our locker; they were two lockers down. Didn't matter; I was committed.

"What kind of sicko would do something like that? Hey! He's still in there! Get out of there, you weirdo!" Gabby crawled out with daggers in his eyes. I had totally thrown him under the bus. While I was melting down and cowardly trying to save myself, one of the adults gave a sideways glance into our locker and said, "Huh." That was it. They couldn't care less what two knuckleheads were doing in the dark. We ran away.

Gabby was always the cool hand Luke in our world. That was not my most impressive day. Amazing, we are still friends. I never went near that locker again. I'm not cut out to be Hugh Heffner. I learned a lesson.

Proverbs 28-1 "The wicked flee even though no one pursues."

Clod Wars

Out behind the apartments, there used to be a large open field. I'd say that field was about 75 yards wide and 150 yards long. It was overgrown with brush and had a catch basin on the far side. A small rise supported a dirt road that ran along the side of the catch basin. Another rise on the near side supported the paved alley driveway that led to the apartments 'underground parking. So the field was kind of a big rectangular casserole dish.

A ton of kids would come out of the family apartment buildings and hang in that field. They were almost exclusively boys. Who else would be drawn to an empty dirt field? We used this battleground for endless afternoon clod fights. The kids would divide up into armies. One side would take the dirt road and the other, the paved road. The object of the war was to cross the field and invade the other army's road. Each side would defend their turf by hurling dirt clods at any enemy kid that tried to cross.

I usually fought for the Paved Army. The bad boys of the apartments usually fought for the Dirt Army. My Noble Paved Army comrades were courageous and excellent marksmen. The Dirt Army warriors were wily and deceitful. They devised a technique of attack that almost won the day for them. They would lob clods in a high arc that took a few seconds to come down. While we watched these ballistic shots fall, they would hurl fastball shots at us while we were distracted. The only thing that saved the day was an all-out counterattack. They had divided their force into ballistic and kinetic throwers. When we came at them screaming, they had no choice but to retreat to their Dirt homeland. It was a costly battle. Several boys got dirty that day. May they lie in the bathtub in peace.

Usually, these battles ended in a stalemate. It was just too dangerous to get close to enemy fire. Yet, the driving competition in us demanded that we come up with technology to overcome the obstacles. Trash can 'shields 'were useful to a point, but they couldn't protect you completely. Plenty of boys got bloody reminders of that when they got so close that fire came from every direction. We needed a way to get close. We found the answer in a Tank. A 'Tank 'was a big refrigerator box with both sides open. Four, sometimes five boys could get in there and crawl it forward, rolling sideways across the field. A few other guys would hide behind the Tank. When we got close enough, everyone would jump out and attack, guns a'blazing.

The day came when we had to put our theories to the test. We procured a huge box that held a side by side freezer from a shady arms dealer (someone's dad). We divided our squad between inside crawlers and outside snipers and launched the attack. I was inside, left. It was hot and dusty in there as we drove our juggernaut forward. Soon, we were in range and began to receive fire. It was exhilarating to hear the clods burst upon our armor while we were safe inside. We got three-quarters of the way across when the Dirts began to panic. They started to throw rocks! ROCKS!

Rocks were outlawed in the Conference of War Treaty of 1968. Nevertheless, the Dirts resorted to stone fire. Typical cheating filthy Dirts! The Tank was well worn and tenderized by our journey, so some of the rocks began to penetrate. Still, we pressed on. It was only when one of our snipers outside screamed, "Brick!" That we knew we had to abandon our Panzer. The incoming brick crushed the box and dug into one guy's back. We all bailed out and ran for cover while a few of our brave Paved snipers covered us.

Well, that killed the war games for a while. Many of the Dirts were remorseful and claimed they were ordered to use rocks by their general, Richard Estes. Estes was the baddest badass of them all. He became our lead singer when we formed our band, The Twilight Twitchers. (Read about that later). But what really killed the games was an invasion that none of us could resist, girls. Girls began to hang around the field. We stopped playing Clod War and began to play Grab Ass. That was a whole different adventure.

Go Cart

If you lived at Bay Village apartments (Torrance) in the mid-late '60s and were a preteen, you probably went to Grace Wright Elementary/Jr. High School. It was within walking distance, out behind Bay Village, east on Spencer, up the hill. I say 'was' because Grace Wright is no longer there. I got razed for a public storage business. Too bad. Lots of great memories there. Every morning during the school year, a column of kids marched up Spencer like refugees. If you listened closely, you could hear the sighs of relief and the clinking of martini glasses from all the adults who finally got a break from the constant kid riot in the apartment buildings. Then, in the afternoon, the tide would turn, and the adults would run for cover. A stampede of brats came charging down the hill to pick up where they left off.

Along the way on Spencer, there was a factory that made little packaged pies, the kind you would put in a paper sack lunch. The smell of baking pie was heavenly. More than a few kids lingered at the little shop that the owner's set up to sell candy, soda, and pies to the walk-by traffic. Sometimes, a pie delivery truck was parked out front with an open back cargo door. We would steal pies with no conscious like seagulls nicking french fries at the pier. I once stole eight pies in one raid and ate them all at once. I celebrated by throwing up up bright red cherries for an hour. That killed it for me.

The more daring boys would wait until one of those trucks was pulling out from the loading dock. As the driver committed to turning down Spencer, they would grab hold of the back bumper to ride down the street, hanging like monkeys a few inches off the asphalt. It looked like fun, but Gabby and I didn't like those odds. We found better odds just down the street.

Running perpendicular to Spencer was Earl. Back then, before developers leveled it out to build condos, Earl was a very steep street with plant nurseries and horse stables on either side. As Gabby and I walked down Spencer from Grace Wright, we heard a commotion. We turned north on Spencer and found a bunch of guys taking turns riding a go-kart down the hill. The metal tube-framed go-kart had no engine, but Earl's steep grade made it go like a bat out of hell downhill. The only problem was that whoever rode the kart down had to drag it back up the hill—no easy chore.

The gang of boys was led by legendary Bay Village badass, Richard Estes. We knew Richard from the open-field clod wars behind the apartments. We asked him if we could take a turn. He said if we served as uphill drag-donkeys for three runs, we would earn a turn to ride. That seemed reasonable. So Gabby and I went down Earl to standby as the next rider came blazing down. When the kart came to a stop, we would each take a side and drag it back up the hill. Then we would return to our station and await the next run. We did this three times. The last rider we donkeyed for was Richard himself. We dragged the kart behind him as he ascended the hill, and he said it was our turn. But not one turn for each of us; we had to go together, then drag it back uphill.

This didn't sit so well with us, but what could we do? Gabby got behind the wheel, and I sat on the engine mount, and we shoved off. When we came over the drop, the kart picked up speed like a meteor entering the atmosphere. Being inches off the ground magnified the thrill. It was a freaking blast, but it was over in seconds. When the kart rolled to a stop, we got out and began the long drag to bring it back uphill.

About two thirds up, inspiration struck. Estes' gang wasn't going to take one step toward us to help with the kart. Gabby hesitated and looked at me. I read his mind. We turned the kart around, I jumped behind the wheel, and Gabby got in back and, zoom! We shot down the hill with Estes' screaming ringing in our ears. When the kart stopped, we dragged it back up. You guessed it. Two-third up, we did it again. This time Richard promised to kick our asses if we didn't return the kart. With sorrowful humility, we dragged the kart back up. No one came to meet us. So... we quickly turned it around and rode down the hill again. This time Richard let go a volley of cussing that would melt the pavement. He sent a crew of henchmen after us. We rode the kart far down Earl, then abandoned it and ran away laughing like hyenas.

We were number one and two on Estes' ass-kicking list for a long time, but we knew how to dodge that Doberman like Chip and Dale. We finally got off his list when we invited him to be the lead singer of my band, the Twilight Twitchers. At least, I think we are off his list. I always look behind me to this day, just in case.

Caveman Romance

When girls started showing up on the field, the dirt clods stopped flying. A virus began to spread. Perfectly normal boys, capable of rowdy mischief-making and violent creativity, suddenly became tame. It didn't happen all at once. At first, it was just a few stragglers, young bucks that strayed too far from the herd that got picked off.

"Hey, our right flank is exposed. What happened to Bowers?"
"He's over there talking to some girl."
"Fine. Who needs him? We still have plenty of guys."

But not for long. The virus was spreading. The battlefield was leaking. Once we lost the critical mass, the war ended. Like me, there remained a few die-hards that kept trying to keep their inner Peter Pan fighting, but it was a losing battle. There is no cure for a girl's freckles.

There was an episode of Star Trek where one by one, everyone in the crew was infected by this flower that would shoot something in their face that would bliss their minds into jelly. It even happened to Spock. This was happening all around me. Even Gabby got infected. Then it infected me, and instantly I went from being Boy Wonder to Pre-Teen Blunder. Didn't matter. My mind was blissed into jelly.

The clods stopped flying. The girls started running around the field. The boys chased them and tackled them. If they were lucky, they would 'accidentally' touch some part of the girl that would ring the bell. They would let the girl up and give her a five-second head start and chase her again. This was the most primitive form of courtship known to man. We were one with our caveman ancestors. All that was missing were the clubs.

At first, I just watched, scoffing and clucking my tongue. Sheesh... The girls were so slow and clumsy. It's like they wanted to be caught. Oh, Ohhhh...

The sun was going down, and the Bay Village Apartment building cast a shadow over the field. Golden rays lit the trees on fire in the distance. Time was running out. Soon we would all have to go home and be kids in our families again. I stood up. I picked out a girl with blond hair. She saw me looking at her, smiled, and bolted. I lunged. She dodged. I stumbled. She spun. I laughed. She took off. I chased. She turned right. I cut her off. She ducked, but I caught her. She fell under me, and I landed to her side with my arm around her chest. She didn't mind. I didn't either. I got on top and held her down for a moment, her hands pinned to the side and her face smiling at me. Adrenaline was shooting out my ears. Now what? I didn't know what to do next, so I gently helped her up, and she ran again.

This went on for a while. I caught and released three girls that afternoon. The first one twice, the second was nice, the third one, yikes! I didn't know any of their names, and they didn't know mine, but we shared this ancient sport with relish. The creaky oak door to a whole new world swung open, even as the door to my innocent childhood swung closed forever.

Ok, girls were on the radar now, but I wasn't too spun up about it. They were confusing to me. I mostly wanted to hang out with Gabby doing monkey business. Gabby was more evolved than I was, so his antenna was always up for a chance to meet girls. I pounded on the closed door to my childhood to let me back in, but it was closed and bolted. A ragged path led away into the dark jungle. Torches lit the way. Drums beat in the distance. The siren song of feral females floated across perfumed air, promising all the danger and adventure a boy could hope for. The dirt field was abandoned, and a new battlefield was open to us—the Party Room.

Born to be Wild

In the Bay Village apartment building, there was a community party room. It was upstairs from the lobby. The decor was Sinatra Swank. It had recessed booths, some tables, chairs, and a large dance floor. Oversized sliding doors opened on a large balcony that overlooked the pool and Jacuzzi. I'm sure that this was the setting for a lot of swinging adult cocktail parties. Beat up parents wondering what happened to their youth would take shelter from the endless riot of brats that swarmed the complex. In the dark, they were players again. I wonder how many divorces were launched there.

Usually, kids weren't allowed up there without adult supervision, but the lobby staff didn't watch too closely. My best friend Gabby and I used to sneak up there and go out on the balcony at night and pitch detergent pods into the Jacuzzi to make it foam up like a giant bubble bath. If any shenanigans were going on in the hot tub, at least they came out spotlessly clean.

Occasionally, there were young teen dance parties up there. Sometimes there was a live band to play music, but mostly it was albums on the stereo. The room was kept dark. The records and disco ball kept spinning. All the pimply-faced voice-crackers would be pressed to the walls and segregated by girls and boys while the Doors tried to light our fires. No one made a move. Everyone ached to break through the thick membrane of awkwardness and get to a release. I guess this is where booze would typically break the ice but (incredibly) no one had any. We had to do it the old fashioned way.

An hour would go by with Steppenwolf screaming we were Born to be Wild while all of us dorks kept to the walls giggling and snickering at each other. Tumbleweeds blew across the dance floor. Then a hero would step forward.

It was NEVER me, and sometimes it never happened. Sometimes, no one made a move all night long until we were finally driven out of the party room back to our apartments. But once in a while, a girl (ALWAYS a girl) would just come over and grab a boy and drag him by his puberty out to the dance floor. Mick Jagger would beg for satisfaction while the sacrificial couple would let the beat invade their bodies. Then they began to move. Stiff and awkward at first, but soon Eric Burden and the Animals would grease their joints, and the pressure would build until the ice cracked. Then exploded. And these heroes would DANCE. Like no one was watching, and no one would find out. Then all the kids would jump through the breach in the wall, and the party would be ON.

With the ice shattered, even I could find a dance partner. My stupid, goofy body would flail in the dark, but I didn't care. The girl I danced with would forgive me with her eyes. For a moment, I would fall in love until the song ended. Then I would fall in love with someone else for the next song. Then a slow song would start, and I would seek out the most merciful girl I could, like Sheryl Weeks. We would cling to each other, rocking back and forth until I had impure ideas. When a night like this happened, I wanted to smash the clocks, shoot the sun, and never let the moment pass.

During one of those dances, I almost married Sheryl on the spot, but something else stole my heart. A snare drum. A dorky teenage band played surf music that night with a low budget drummer who had one snare drum with a cymbal attached to the side. It was the bitchenest thing I had ever seen. I wanted it so bad. The dude playing it even let me wail on it for a while he made a move on Sheryl. Sorry, Sheryl, you were dead to me at that moment. If you're a drummer, you understand. I was infected with musician's disease from that moment on.

Alas, nothing lasts forever. Too soon, the adults came to stop the music, turn on the glaring lights, and burst the bubble. We all climbed back into our protective membranes, acted like none of it happened, and faded away home. But not before Gabby and I pitched another detergent pod in the Jacuzzi.

The Twilight Twitchers

I could hardly sleep. Being in the driver's seat to a rocking song was drummer's crack. The next day, I found the same snare and cymbal duo at the TG&Y on Anza. I silently pledged my heart to it and promised it I would beg my mom and Dad to get it for me for Christmas. I pitched the idea like a screenwriter with no conscious. Of course, they said it couldn't be done, no way, not in a million years, not even if a gun were held to their head. I smiled. That usually means it's a sure thing. Still, I detected a note of painful angst in my mom's eyes that bespoke the fact that we were probably too poor to get a big thing like that. They kept redirecting me to other, cheaper alternatives like a Johnny 7 Gun or a Man from U.N.C.L.E. attaché case with five secret weapons. I didn't want any of that crap but faced with her insistence; I pretty much figured my dream was D.O.A.

When Christmas finally came, I woke up at 5 am. Everyone else was asleep. I wandered out to the living room. It was lit by the soft glow of Christmas tree lights, sparkling through the tinsel. In the half-dark, there was a full drum kit: blue sparkle bass, toms, snare, high hat, and cymbals. The sight stunned me, rocked me back, and I think a little pee came out. I stood there, speechless. I moved in closer, but I didn't touch it for fear that I would burst the sweetest dream I ever had. Instead, I just curled up on the sofa and stared at it until the rest of my family woke up.

That lasted for 5 minutes. Then I went and woke everyone up and dragged them into the living room. My mom cried at my excitement. My Dad warned me that these drums were not toys, and I should take care of them. My older sisters had 'WTF 'all over their faces as they realized the family wad was blown on their brother. They inspected their new socks and sweaters like they were dead rats. My little sister Syndie didn't care; she was drunk on new Barbie swag. It was the best Christmas of my life.

I rewarded my family's love by learning to drum behind 2 inch walls. For the next month, I tortured everyone until I could lay down that surf beat ('boom-tat-tat-boom-tat, boom-tat-tat-boom-tat), reliably enough to join a band. You could hardly call it a band. We had one guy, Marc, who could play pretty good lead guitar, another kid John, who beat power chords out of a worn out Fender Telly that's probably worth more than my car now, and me with my sparkly Japanese drums. Our front man was the 12-year-old badass General from the Dirt Army, Richard Estes. We made him our singer because we were all afraid of him. We were the 'Twilight Twitchers. 'I still can't say that without laughing.

We were serious about the music, maaan. As serious as we could be at 11-12 years old. We played a lot of surf music—the Ventures, Dick Dale, Surfaries and so on. I was famous among my pimply peers for my rendition of 'Wipe Out. 'I also kicked ass on the theme from 'Hawaii Five-O. 'We covered some Steppenwolf, Doors, and Iron Butterfly. Totally eclectic, don't you think? We did. We played a regular gig at our party room for all the other pre-teen geeks. Sheryl got over me. I was married to my sticks now. But our high watermark came when we got a paying gig for a dance at a club a few blocks away.

For the princely sum of $50, the Twilight Twitchers hit the road. I piled all my drum set in a shopping cart and pushed it a mile down Torrance Blvd. to an A.F.W. hall. We set up, and soon the crowd began to pour in. They were all mentally disabled people. Hmm... alrighty then.

We launched into our set. We played everything we knew. I sparkled on my solo during 'In-A-Gadda-Da-Vida". 'I played so hard my bass drum kept creeping away across the linoleum floor. I had to stretch like a gymnast to keep up until someone pushed it back in. We closed with 'Little Red Riding Hood, 'Estes's favorite and a tune that kills at the party room in Bay Village. It flopped. Crickets. The natives were getting restless.

Then one handicapped guy asked if we could play the theme to the Batman TV show. You know, 'DA DA-da da-(da da)- da da- DA DA- da da- (da da)- da da- BAT-MAAAN! 'Sure, we can play it. It's just a surf beat with a lead guitar line and a crunch from our other guitar. Estes even knew the words! So do you! He sang it. They loved it. They all danced and spun and gyrated in strange handicapped abandon. We played it over and over again. The natives went wild with delight. We laughed so hard, our ribs ached.

Eventually, we had to stop, or they would have all had strokes. They all surrounded Estes and wanted to make him their God. We got our money from a nice lady with horn-rim glasses who said we were the best band they ever had. Estes put the cash in his pocket, and we never saw it again. Still, we were on our way. Look out, Beatles, here come the Twilight Twitchers!

Alas, a story old as time itself, our band could not deal with success, and we broke up. The Twilight Twitchers faded into history. All that's left are bitter-sweet memories and ringing in the ears. In a stroke of beautiful irony, I grew up to have a son who is a member of that magical autism tribe. And he loves music as well. James was a regular on stage with me at our church's worship service for over two decades. I'm a bass player now, but James is the one who keeps us grounded. He's the one who lights the fire of the Holy Spirit. Ask anyone in my church.

To this day, when I'm at a concert, no matter what kind of band is playing; Rock, Bluegrass, Classical, Mariachi, whatever, I wait for a lull in the noise, and I shout out a request for 'In-A-Gadda-Da-Vida'. It always gets a laugh. Sometimes they even try to play it. I smile and think of the Twilight Twitchers.

Paper Route

My musical career was on hold, so I needed a day job. I became a delivery boy for the Herald Examiner. I delivered to all the apartment buildings on Anza Ave. Sadly, I was terrible. I was late, sometimes threw the paper on the roof, or just forgot customers. I was eleven years old. I was new to work, I hadn't learned to care yet, but I still liked it. I liked the money, the feeling of independence. I had a big ink-stained canvas saddle bag to hang on my Stingray handlebars, each side filled with papers that I had to fold beforehand. Every day, I would load up and make my rounds in the afternoons. The exception to this was Sunday, when I had to deliver the big paper in the morning.

One Sunday morning, I was up at 3 am waiting for the paper bundle to arrive. I watched 'A Midsummer Night's Dream' on the only channel broadcasting at that time of night (KHJ 9). All the rest (2,4,5,7,11,13) were off the air or had the Indian logo test pattern running. Once again, I wondered why I got myself into this job while I sat in my living room, lit only by the TV, trying to wake up while all the rest of my family slept. I had to keep checking the drop point outside, five apartments down, outside the lobby. It was very cold (by California standards), about 55 degrees.

The movie was over, so I checked the drop for the fourth time, and the bundle was finally there. I dragged the heavy bundle back to my apartment and started folding and tying the papers and stuffing them into my saddlebag. It was about 4:30 am when

I left the apartment bearing my load over my shoulders and walked down to where my Stingray was locked. I got the bag hung over the handlebars and took off.

Anza Ave always seemed like Broadway to me. It was always jam-packed with traffic. At this wee hour, it was deserted. I rode my bike out into the middle of the street and made lazy s's across all the lanes. I felt like Charlton Heston in 'The Last Man on Earth.' Eventually, I got to the first building on my route and started my rounds. The quiet, the solitude, the night air cast a spell. I became filled with gratitude for the responsibility and privilege of being up so early when everyone else was still tucked under the covers. I didn't screw around that morning. I hand placed each big paper right in front of the door it belonged to like I was a stork delivering babies.

By the time I got to the end of the route, morning had broken, and I wasn't alone anymore. Traffic had begun to occupy Anza. I stopped at a convenience store at the end of my block and bought a hot chocolate (I didn't drink coffee yet) and a donut. I sat on the corner outside the store and thought about all the people who were waking up, going out to fetch their papers, and sitting in their kitchens reading over a hot cup of coffee. I felt good that I had played a small part in making life in my hometown, just a little sweeter. When I got home, my mom gave me a kiss and let me sleep in till 10.

Everyone needs to taste the nectar of responsibility once in a while. It isn't always about the money. There is magic in the work, if you look for it.

Mall Rats

If you roll south down Anza from the Bay Village Apartments to Torrance Blvd, then turn east, you will get to Hawthorne Blvd in a few blocks. This is the main back artery for the South Bay. Working with my dad, I traveled this fabled spice route between dicey Inglewood in the north and swarthy San Pedro in the south many times. There were shopping centers all along the route, like Moroccan Bazaars. In later years, the experimental Old Towne Mall would be built. It was an enclosed mall built to look like a town from 1900's Americana. That was yet to come, and it shows up prominently in my teen years, but at this moment in time, the Del Amo Shopping center was the magnet that pulled all the mall rats from Bay Village to swarm its goods and wares. Gabby and I worked this circuit.

Del Amo Mall was the biggest indoor Mall in the US for a while until the Mall of America was built in the mid-west. It had every kind of store, restaurant, and amusement in it. Gabby and I made a playground out of it. At Woolworths, we would screw around with the merchandise. We would set all the manual alarm clocks on the table to go off at the same time. We would position the dolls and stuffed animals in compromising positions. We would drop odd things in people's shopping carts when they weren't looking. Sometimes we would follow people as they walked so closely that we would walk inside their steps. We were just annoying punks. Remember the pop-tops on soda cans that came off? We would work the tab off the little ring and then use it to shoot the ring like a little Frisbee. People were nothing but targets for our shooting gallery. The best fun was 'no-limit' tag. When we played tag, no part of the Mall was off-limits. Our chases led through back areas of shops, through restaurants, over displays, and anywhere a kid could get into. But the best thing about Del Amo was girls.

In '68, I was an eleven-year-old chunky punk, and Gabby was a skinny rat. I looked like a dork; Gabby was hideous. We were Laurel and Hardy as pimply-faced pre-teen knuckleheads. What girl would come close to us if it weren't for the concrete walls that enclosed the Mall? At the Mall, they couldn't get away. So we stalked them, annoyed them, pissed them off, and secretly tried to figure them out.

Gabby and I started a game of Mall ditch one day. I was 'It,' and he was the prey, so he left me sitting on a bench near the Aladdin's Castle on the lower level. I was supposed to count to 100 before beginning the hunt. This would end in a no-holds-barred chase once I found him. While I was counting down, a clutch of girls walked past me, and I became mesmerized by one of them. She was wearing a paisley patterned blouse open at the neck a few buttons with super big collar tips that touched her outside shoulders (remember those?). The blouse was untucked and breezed over a fairly short mini skirt. Glossy white boots and a French beret set off a very 'mod' look. I didn't understand her Nuevo-retro fashion statement then; I just thought she was 'Groovy'. The hook didn't set until she looked my way and smiled at me. Gabby? Who's Gabby?

I followed her group up the stairs at a discreet distance. She walked with an easy grace and just owned her look. Her friends were just average girls, but she was the rebel in the group. Her soulful stride demanded you get on board or get out of the way. I wanted to buy a ticket to ride, but I was just a dork. I thought about letting go, but she kept tossing me these glances that said, "Are you coming?" At least, I think that's what I heard in my head.

The group went into a chic store (the Gap?), and I sat on a bench outside to wait and watch. I looked to see if Gabby was around. No, thank God. The last thing I need is for him to burst my bubble. From my seat on the bench, I tried to look inside the shop and see her. She wasn't visible, but other girls were. They were pulling blouses off racks and looking over the jeans and so on. The thought lit up; 'they are doing it for ME'. Well, not me specifically, but to make themselves attractive to guys. Huh.. I'M a guy! Their team is working hard for MY team. What a gift! Girls actually want to radiate attractiveness. Guys don't care so much. When I put on clothes, I'm only thinking about how well I can move; how comfortable they are. I never gave any thought about being 'attractive'. Of course, that would explain a lot. Suddenly I was aware of my t-shirt and jeans and felt like I could do better.

Mod Girl and her posse stepped out of the shop in mid-thought. They turned my way. I wanted to run, but it was too late. They were bearing down on my position, and Mod Girl was staring me down. Smiling. Floating like a summer breeze. I couldn't look away. I was a deer in the beautiful headlights. She was the 'Girl from Ipanema'. As she came closer, I could see she was several years older than me. Maybe a junior or senior at High School while I was still trapped behind the wall of Jr. High. She was out of my reach, untouchable. Yet, as she passed, she reached out and touched my head as if to whisper, "Tag, your IT. Now CHASE me". One last smile, tossed over her shoulder, and she disappeared in the crowd.

My head exploded. I sat on that bench with surges of electricity tingling my fingers. That touch was her saying, "thank you for appreciating me". She loved that I enjoyed her presence, her beauty. Even though I was too young to matter, I validated her effort. I determined right there that I would try to do better than a t-shirt and jeans. I never saw that girl again, but The Chase had begun.

It took me until my late twenties to catch up to an exotic flower. When I did, I married Susan, and we have been together nearly forty years now. Ahh... the best thirty years of my life.

(P.S. I'm writing this piece right now wearing a t-shirt and jeans.)

Over the Line

Work was still a concept I held lightly in my hand. What I took seriously was fun. My best friend, Gabby, had a remarkable gift in making friends that I couldn't touch with a ten-foot pole. I was a social cripple by comparison. We favored each other's company because we shared the same loony view of life. We could make a game out of anything. Then we would compete over it like it was a gladiatorial death-match. The stakes were always high. The loser would have to grovel on their knees across the atrium of the Del Amo mall while they sang the of the glory of the winner, or something else as humiliating. I don't know what was more fun, winning, or losing. We had no shame, so making an ass out of ourselves in public was pure sport.

For a very short time, Gabby and I got into playing over-the-line baseball. I know that there are rules to this game, and it is played on club levels, but Gabby and I couldn't care a butt hair about that. We just made up rules as we went. Gabby knew a gang of other friends he could pull together to meet on a grass field to play. We would divide up whoever showed up and mark out lines with t-shirts, pop bottles, whatever was handy. Then we would toss the ball up and try to swat it past the other boys ready with their gloves. This was as close to an actual sport I ever got by that time. It was a blast. The trash-talking alone was worthy of the bluest standup comedians in Hollywood. It's hilarious to turn a pack of pre-teen boys loose to insult each other with vulgar references and motifs that Facebook would not allow to be posted in today's politically sensitive era. Sometimes we would fall over holding our sides, laughing our butts off.

It was during one of these games that I had an epiphany. I wouldn't know to call it that at the time, but it stayed with me all these years. It happened during a late spring afternoon in '68 when the sun broke through after a week of rain. The sky was filled with crisp little clouds floating in neon blue. The air was scrubbed of its usual smog, and the temperature was perfect. We were out playing Over-the-Line with the guys, and I was deep in the outfield. It hit me; what if this is as good as life gets? At that age, I didn't carry the burden of an adult; I wasn't aware of the world's troubles; my heart was still unbroken and full of silly hope. I thought life would undoubtedly become more colorful, filled with better toys, more exotic adventures, romance, achievement, and triumph but will it ever be BETTER than this?

Gabby and I carried our Over-the-Line game with us into the wild. We would go to a stream bed on camping trips and find an appropriate log to serve as a bat and swat rocks for hours. We would improvise a little diamond in the sand to track base movement and then swing for the fences. We each had three outs an inning. A swing and a miss was an out. If a rock didn't cross the water, it was a ground-out. A bounce into the water was a single, hitting the ground across the water was a double, into the bush past the water was a triple and over the brush was over the fence for a home run. Pebbles would move around the bases, and the score was scratched in the dirt. We would supply the play by play and ramp up the drama of each at-bat. Of course, the trash talk could peel the paint from a battleship. Playing OTL with rocks, or finger football with folded triangles of paper was never a waste of time.

One weekend we were bored, so we made our own Foosball table out of plywood and dowels and hand-carved the 'players'. My team was the Tijuana Tigers, Gabby's was the Ensenada Enchiladas. I gave my 'forward' the most macho phallic name I could think of. Penis Rodriguez. Gabby named his players the same way. I don't remember all the hilarious names we came up with, but I can't forget Harry Scrotum, Rod Bonerman, and Seymour Snatchez. Eleven-year-olds. Sheesh! There was no video game technology back then; only the gray crap between your ears to work with. We sucked the marrow from the bone.

I tried to infect my own kids with this hyper-competitive virus, but it didn't take. My oldest daughter didn't care enough, James was too sweet, and my youngest couldn't stand the trash talk heat. Oh, well. When I go for a walk in the woods, I still have an eye out for a suitable log and a bed of stones. It's always a beautiful day for a ballgame.

A Date for Disneyland

My family was not rich. That's an understatement. I never thought of us as being poor, but lavish spending was not an option. So, imagine my excitement when my Dad announced at breakfast that we were all going to Disneyland. On top of that, we could each take a friend. My head nearly exploded.

Disneyland was about the most wonderful thing that could happen to a kid. Heck, every Sunday night, Walt Disney himself would torture us with glimpses of Disneyland on the TV. For a family like mine, that seemed as far removed as Buckingham Palace. We had been to POP and Knott's Berry Farm in Buena Park but as sweet as they were, Disneyland was the Grand Daddy of the All. I don't know who my Dad had to kill to get tickets, but God bless them, and may they rest in peace.

Getting to the big D was over the moon, but getting to take my best friend Gabby just supercharged the possibilities. We already knew how to make fun out of just about any boring situation, and now we would have the greatest canvass in the world for our art. We would prank our way down Main Street, go ape crazy in the Jungle Cruise, swash our buckles at the Pirates of the Caribbean and drop spit bombs from the Gondola Ride. The elders would sing of this day around the tribal fires and re-enact our antics dressed in ceremonial costumes representing The Legendary

Lawler and Hayse. Men would crow, women would weep, and children would dream.

It was 9 am. We were leaving at 11 am. I got on the phone and called Gabby's house. No answer. I went next door and knocked. No answer. Of all days! Now he disappears? I swallowed a lump of panic and walked around the apartment complex. I asked a few kids if they had seen him, but no dice. I went home to wait. Maybe he just went to breakfast at Sambo's or something. He'll be back. He can't miss this epic opportunity. Just stay calm.

9:45 am
My sister's had already lined up their best girlfriends. They were busy getting dressing for the boys they might meet there. My oldest pre-hippy sister Margie was bringing one of her stoner friends. I'm sure the pharmaceuticals will be flowing. My next oldest sister Kate was bringing Sheryl Weeks. Now that babe was very easy on the eyes. She even smiles at me now and then. There were possibilities there. I'm not saying we were a thing, but you never know. I wouldn't mind sitting behind her on the Matterhorn. A man has to hold onto something while careening through the mountain, doesn't he? What happens in Disneyland - stays in Disneyland.

Mom asked me, "Who are you taking?" I snapped off a decisive, "Gabby!" "Oh, you two will have a great time, honey," she replied. I smiled, but inside I thought 'OF COURSE we will have a great time. A LEGENDARY TIME.' I started getting ready. T-shirt, button-down top shirt with breast pockets for all the "E" ticket books, jeans, and sensible tennis shoes. I'm ready for action. Still, no Gabby.

10:30 am

I repeated the search pattern. No answer when I call. Silent as the grave when I knock on his door. Nobody knows nothing. The anxiety is wasting me. This epic opportunity is shrinking down to a hard, bitter disappointment. I'm getting angry with Gabby. What the hell are you doing that could be better than this?

11 am

El Jack is punctual if nothing else, so he cracks the whip to get everyone out the door. I make one last call, but I know it's no use. As we drive off, I look back one last time and then surrender. I spill my dreams like an armload of plates on the floor. Sheryl Weeks isn't even looking at me. I can't hang with her now; I'm a third wheel. You have to go with even numbers, or the ride seating just exposes your desperation. I'm going to be a lost soul, wandering around by myself like a skunk.

When we enter the main gate and start to walk down Main Street, my older sisters split off and head for the rides. I'm stuck with my little 6year old sister Syndie and my Mom and Dad. Before I could run away, here comes Mickey Mouse. Syndie screamed in delight. She ran up and gave the mouse a big hug. I can't help but smile. Donald Duck is right behind Mickey. Syndie is flipping out as only a six-year-old can. Then I realize this is her first time in Disneyland, old enough to understand what it's all about. She is gushing about it to me. She doesn't want to be under Mommy and Daddy's shadow; she wants to be with me. Her eyes beg me to be her best friend today, to spend this wonderful day showing her the big D like she was a big girl.

"Mom, can I take Syndie to Fantasyland?" I hear myself ask.
"Sure, honey. Just meet us in front of the castle at 3 pm."

Mom and Dad grab the golden ring of time alone and split before I could reconsider. So I spent the day discovering Peter Pan, Pinocchio, Mr. Toad, and Snow White through the eyes of my cute little curly blond date like it was the first time. She made me six years old again. I laughed and ran and went wild with such abandon; I believe we wrung more fun out of that place than whatever Gabby and I could have. When we floated past the hippos in the Jungle Cruise, she held me tight. I showed her all the secret passageways through the caves on Tom Sawyer's Island. We sang the whole way through 'It's a Small World.' She sat on my shoulders to see the parade and screamed out every character's name as they went by. We took in the whole Disneyland experience like two sailors on shore leave in New York. I earned such loving looks from my little sister that it even washed Sheryl Weeks from my mind. Syndie knighted me Best Big Brother Forever.

When we finally made that final, bitter-sweet march down Main Street past the trees all lit with twinkling lights, Syndie's little hand was in mine. She slept with her head in my lap the whole way home, dreaming of the Happiest Place on Earth. Then I knew why God had fed pancakes to Gabby at Sambo's that morning. I had a different kind of epic to write that day.

The Call of the Sea

The go-to beach destination for most of us living in the Bay Village apartments was the Redondo Beach Pier and King Harbor. We knew how to get there (straight west down Torrance Blvd), and it was full of all kinds of fun. We were still a bit young to dial into the 'lay on the beach watching girls in bikinis' groove, and we didn't surf. Those bronze dudes from Hermosa and Manhattan were still a different species to us. Keep your 'Gidget and Moondoggie'; we were looking for more of a 'Coney Island' experience. The horseshoe pier at Redondo came close.

The Horseshoe Pier (part of King Harbor) ran out over the water, past the surf break, and returned in a half-circle. There was a small spur that accommodated fishermen. Greasy people dropped lines from greasy pier rails and pulled up mackerel, bonito, bat rays, and other hideous bottom feeders. The rest of it was a tourist destination like you would find on the boardwalk in Atlantic City. I think they even sold saltwater taffy there.

There were lots of little shops on the pier itself along with Hot Dog on a Stick type eateries. The Breakers restaurant sat out on the pilings over the water on the north side. It seemed like the swanky haunt of 007 to me. It was a fixture there before it burned down in '88. My mom worked there as a waitress for a while.

Inside the horseshoe, there was a beach with a reasonable break for body surfing. It was a good place to learn. The advantage there was you could properly judge the size of the set coming in as it passed the pier footings in front of you. It was also fun to jump off that pier and swim in. I spent more than a few days at that little beach clowning around with Gabby.

Off to the north of the pier was a small breakwater comprised of huge boulders, protecting the inner harbor. The spaces between this breakwater's boulders formed lots of caves and secret passageways that we crawled around in like rats.

The inner harbor basin was surrounded by little shops with a fish market on one side and a funky bar on the other. The bar was cool. It had a menagerie of nautical stuff all over the walls and ceiling. Later it became a fun zone with arcade games. The thing that fascinated me was the basin itself. The water was usually very clear, and when the sun was just right, the whole bottom was lit up. I could stand at the rail and look down and see octopus, crabs, and all kinds of fish.

As impressive as all this was, my gang of wharf rats wasn't there for the tourist attractions. We had a mission. We intended to rent a rowboat for a few hours and row all the way to the wreck of the Dominator off Palos Verdes. The rusty hull of the Dominator was clearly visible to everyone in the South Bay for years because it was silhouetted against the blue sky just off the point. We imagined there would be booty to be had if we could just get there. It was only ten miles or so over the open sea. No problem, right?

When we paid the man for the rowboat, he made sure to tell us to stay in the harbor. We all gave each other a knowing wink and agreed. We piled into the boat with our sack lunches and bottles of Pepsi, ready for adventure. There were two oars, so two guys each got one, and we set out. Everyone started arguing over the oars, and we couldn't get them coordinated. The distant image of the Dominator beckoned past the breakwater just dripping with riches, but progress was slow. We managed to get close enough to the mouth of the harbor to start feeling the ocean waves, but we couldn't get out. All we did was row around in circles behind the breakwater until I was so seasick I wanted to die. My 'faithful crew' thought it was soo funny. They finally ditched me on the wharf where I lay in my vomit. Marooned there, I watched the other guys splash around until some others got seasick and started chumming the water. They abandoned the Dominator and tried to get back to the dock, but the tide was running out. Finally, a man had to go out in a boat with an outboard and tow them in. We all lay on the wharf like a haul of tuna, moaning, and vomiting for an hour. So much for the call of the sea. Can you imagine eight 11-year-olds rowing through 10 miles of open ocean? Oh, well... a boy can dream, can't he?

Fish Tale

One Saturday, El Jack woke me up early. The sun wasn't quite up yet. He told me Johnny (his younger brother) would be here any minute. I had to get dressed, make a lunch, and an extra sandwich to eat on the way. El Jack was all business when he was on an expedition. I had to snap to it or get left behind. His little brother, my Uncle Johnny, had agreed to take my Dad and I out fishing on the Isle of Redondo, a stationary barge that used to be anchored off the coast of Redondo Beach.

My Uncle Johnny just got out of prison (I never knew what he was in for), and he was devouring life like a man brought to a buffet from years in the desert. He was prison hard, not the warm, loving Uncle you would wish for. I always felt like he would kill me for my lunch money if he had a chance. My Dad, his older brother, loved him and tried hard to fold him into normal family life. But Johnny was wild at heart. It seemed like he could blow anytime. My Dad was the rod in the reactor that kept him reasonably cool. Johnny was the fisherman in the family, so this was his expedition.

We pulled into a parking lot. King Harbor, back then, was just a smelly little nest of beat-up boats rocking gently against the moorings. The smell of salt air mixed with tar and rotting fish was intoxicating. It smelled like adventure. It was then that we found out that we weren't taking the ferry to the Isle; we were going out on a private half day boat with some other guys. I wasn't crazy about this plan because I get dreadfully seasick on the open water. I was looking forward to the relative stability of the barge to mute the rocking. I mentioned this to my Dad, but his answer was to give me some Dramamine while we walked out to find the boat. "Aren't you supposed to take this an hour before?" I asked, apparently to myself. Dad ignored me. He did not want me to show up like a pussy to his brother. We walked out on the docks to find the boat.

We found it. It was an old Chris Craft that reminded me of the 'Minnow,' the doomed boat from Gilligan's Island. It had peeling paint and barnacles crusting the bottom. We were the last to get there, so we shoved off as soon as we were aboard. It had about ten guys on it altogether, including the captain and one guy who was the crew. I don't know who the other guys were. One or two knew my Uncle Johnny but the others seemed to be friends of the captain.

We ran about an hour out, past the Isle of Redondo to someplace that had a name (which I don't remember) but looked like any other spot on the sea. Everyone dropped lines in the water around the boat. Nothing was happening, and I was fighting to keep from thinking of the rocking waves, so I got my lunch out. I opened my bag to get some potato chips, and Uncle Johnny grabbed the bag from behind. "What's this? A BANANA?" He threw the whole bag overboard. I looked at my Dad, but he just shrugged. Johnny went on, "bananas are bad luck. NEVER bring a banana on a boat."

Is that a thing? I didn't know that. Why did he have to throw my whole lunch out? That sandwich I made was a masterpiece. He said it had to go because everything had touched the banana.

Everyone agreed. I found out that fishermen are more superstitious than baseball players. They had all kinds of weird restrictions. Seemed stupid to me, but the fish started biting almost right away.

A school of Bonita was under us, and everyone was hooking up, even me. I had one on my line, reeling him in when another fisherman came around fighting with something big and cut my line to get around me. Really? That happened twice. I complained to my Dad, but he just told me to put another hook on.

The Bonita run was over, so my Dad put a heavy sinker on my line and told me to go for the bottom, maybe get a rockfish or something. I hooked something. I didn't think it was a fish because there was no action on the line. It was just heavy to reel in. After a long time reeling, I saw something coming up from the bottom. It looked like a coffee table. When it got to the surface, my Uncle got a pole-jig and hooked a weird flat fish like a halibut. It was huge. It flapped lazily on the deck like it was bored. I was the man of the hour for all the trouble. I had caught the biggest fish that day.

The crew guy offered to 'dress' it, and I said sure. He sliced it up, cleaned it, and cut the meat out of it in the deckhouse while I tried to catch another. When he came out, he gave me a plastic bag with a few pieces of fish. "That's all that came out of that big thing?" I asked my Dad. Uncle Johnny had 'words' with the captain. I don't know what he said but out came three bags as big as the one they gave me. Sometimes it's useful to know a badass. Seasickness was setting in as we got back. It reminded me that I don't have the inner ear to be a blue water fisherman, but I sure love to eat it. I wish I still had that sandwich.

Ballistics

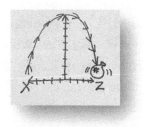

I have always had a fascination for ballistics. Ever since I saw John Wayne hurl a grenade over enemy lines in 'Sands of Iwo Jima', I wanted to be the one who could reach the target from a high arc. Gabby and I made great use of our ballistic aptitude in our apartment building.

The Bay Village apartments were planted throughout with olive trees. There was an abundance of olives all around on the ground. We would grab a handful as we walked and fire a ballistic volley at any kid that crossed our path. They would fire back. In this way, we honed our skills. Of course, firing an olive directly at a person is always a good choice. If you had reasonable aim and velocity, you can hit anyone in a twenty to thirty foot range. But, the real challenge was to lob a handful and aim for a spot where your target would be when the volley came down. This required mathematic instincts. Thank God I didn't know math was involved back then, or I would have lost interest immediately.

The other great advantage with artillery was that you can hide from your target, and they would never know where the hell was raining down from. We took this advantage to a near-fatal end. We hid behind a cinder block wall that surrounded Bay Village and faced Anza Ave. Anza was a pretty bust street with lots of cars driving by. They were going pretty fast, and it was proving impossible to zero in, one olive at a time. We got frustrated and decided to fire handfuls at a time. We still missed. Finally, we decided to fire at the same time, about fifteen olives each. Surely at least one or two olives would hit the target. A car approached. We crouched behind the wall. Gabby called the shot. Fire! We released simultaneously. The cluster arced over the wall and came down perfectly on the windshield of the passing car. 'Brrrrrraapppp!' went to olives. The car hit the brakes, skidded out of control, and almost jumped the curb. It came to rest at a cockeyed angle in the middle of the street, stopping traffic. A man hot for blood came out of the car a searched for someone to kill. We hid behind the wall and didn't breathe. At last, he gave up and got back in and drove off. That ended our olive terrorism but not my love for ballistics.

Dirt clods have always been a kid's stand-in for grenades. I think it's the way a clod would hit the ground from on high and explode in all directions. It was delightfully satisfying. We used to have tremendous clod fights out in the field behind the apartments. I wrote about one such battle a few chapters before. My eye was always keen for a beautifully packed dirt clod.

I assumed that everyone loved the spectacle of a dirt clod explosion. Anytime I could provide one for public review, I was ready for the judges. I got a chance out by Del Amo Mall that ended my career as a public clod artist.

Gabby and I were on our way to terrorize Del Amo, and we got stuck at the intersection of Hawthorn Blvd. and Carson Street, where the big Union Bank building looked out towards the Mall. While waiting for the light to change, I noticed a few choice dirt clods in the planter by the sidewalk. They were nicely shaped, orange-sized, tightly packed grenades of semi-dried mud. Who could resist? I picked one up in my hand and hefted its weight.

Perfect! Not too light, so a lob felt silly but not so heavy that it would strain a muscle while casting overhead. I lobbed one in toward the greenway in front of the bank. It hit the grass with a small burst that was just embarrassing. That ground was too soft. I turned my eyes to the street. All the cars were stopped in all four directions. Everyone was facing the middle of a completely empty intersection. Just what I need; a captive audience. I felt for the wind, focused on the middle of the 'arena' and heard Gabby start to say, "Lawler, don't...." when I let loose a high arcing lob for all the people to see and enjoy.

My ballistic math was juuust a bit off. The clod came down on the front hood of a nice Lincoln in front of me. It hit with a satisfying 'Kump', and send clod shrapnel splashing in all directions in a ten-foot radius. I'm sure it left a dent on his hood. Down deep inside me, I felt happy-flappy with my work. Out on the surface, my eyes bugged out, and my heart jumped out of my throat. The man whose car I beaned got out, enraged. Gabby ran for his future. My feet were stuck to the pavement. I said I was sorry, but I don't think he could hear me over all the cussing. The ONLY thing that saved me was the light that turned green, the honking of the other cars, and the thought of showering in prison for child-slaughter that must have entered the man's mind. He got back in his car and drove off.

I found Gabby, and we debriefed about the inci-dent (see what I did there?). We both agreed that we still loved ballistics, but we needed less destructive ammunition to exercise our passion—water balloons.

Back at the apartment, no group of kids was safe. If we heard a gaggle of kid noise around the corner, we would load up and fire a volley of water balloons over the wall and listen for their reaction. I learned that it's best to fire a few dead center then immediately fire another volley a bit to either side to hit those who ran away. This was better than sex to me. Of course, I hadn't had sex yet, but I was pretty sure hitting strangers with water balloons was bitchen. We took our artillery skills on the road.

Just south of the horseshoe pier at Redondo, the beach is laid out below a bluff where Esplanade runs between the alphabet avenues until it reaches the Riviera. This set up was made for artillery. You can see lots of targets (people) laying out on the sand below, just waiting to be bombarded from that bluff. Who wouldn't want to be hit with a two-pound ball of water from 50 feet above? I see the problem now, but I didn't see it then. We fired volley after volley, but we couldn't hit anyone. I think God was pushing our water balloons aside to save lives. We couldn't get our shots much past the strand below, and eventually, we ran out of balloons. Thank God.

Well, I'm a grown man now living peaceful-like on my sleepy street in Whittier, just minding my own business. Oh, and did I mention? We have a bunch of kids on this street.

They cluster together sometimes.

They make noise I can zero in on.

I got a hose.

I got balloons.

"Incoming!!!"

"Heads up!"

 During this time in Torrance, girls began to move in on my mind like a herd of cattle wandering into a western town. Pretty soon, I couldn't think of anything without knocking over a girl thought. I'd watch Saturday morning cartoons like I have all my life, but now I'm noticing how different Wilma looked compared to Fred Flintstone. II even began to prefer Betty Rubble over Wilma. Am I the only one going nuts here? I don't think so.

Now, I am the only boy in my family, besides my Dad. I have three sisters, a Mom, and a Grandma to deal with, so I know a little about women. But now that I'm turning 12, there was this whole other thing opening up about women I knew nothing about. It's exciting, frightening, and crazy-making, and I want to know more. My two older sisters tried to take me under their wing and teach me.

I didn't have any friends that were girls. Linda, the smoking mistress of the Bay Village Apartments, had moved away. All the girls I had tackled in the field out back were nameless conquests I never spoke to again. The only chance I had to talk to any girls was when one of my sister's friends came over. That is how I met my first crush, Sheryl.

Our apartment was an upstairs unit accessed by a long, narrow stairway when you opened the front door. My sisters began to hang out on those stairs with their friends. They let me hang around if I didn't act like a punk, so I got to study girls up close and listen to them talk. It was fascinating.

My sisters are girls, of course, but they don't count. Yet their friends were something very different. Each one packed a potential for infantile romance. Some of the friends were just annoying or had no spark of attraction, but a few positively hummed with chemistry. Sheryl was like that. We would sit on those stairs for hours so close I learned her smell. I watched her when she talked to my sister Kate. Her manner was feminine. Her long blond hair was feminine. Even her skin, her shape, her movements, and the sound of her voice was feminine. That is when I realized that girls were a completely different species than boys. I felt a longing, like a gravitational pull, to be with her. I said nothing. I thought I was keeping cool and aloof, but everything but my voice begged for her attention.

My sister saw it. So did Sheryl. With my big sister's tacit approval, Sheryl sort of opened the door. She let it be known that she 'liked' me. That was a real sizzler on the gossip grid. Soon everyone in our apartment building knew about it. At this point, I hadn't even touched her or spoken directly to her, but the 'going steady' bells were about to ring. With all this pressure from within to be with her, and the expectation and blessing from our stairwell group, I figured it was time to consummate our 'steadiness' somehow. I had to do something that would make it clear that Sheryl and I were 'an item.' I made my move on the stairs.

We all sat on different steps. There were about eight of us there. Sheryl sat on my side, one step higher than me. I sat RIGHT NEXT TO HER! It's hard to explain how blatant this was to me.

I was coming out now. No going back. Everyone knew this was a big moment for us. The springs of tension would up. They all looked excitedly to see what would happen next. Sheryl's back was flat against the wall, and she was one step higher than me. I wanted to make my move. I raised my arm to put it around her, thereby claiming her as my official girlfriend, but I couldn't get it behind her the way we were sitting. There I was, with my arm in the air and everyone holding their breath to see us become as one. Sheryl was smiling, but her head was against the wall. I couldn't get in there without prying her off the wall. What to do, what to do. Aha! I've got it! I put my arm against the wall above her head, and half asked/ half commanded, "Head Up?!"

Ugh! Even now, it sounds so awkward and stupid; no wonder everyone burst out laughing. Even Sheryl had to snicker a little. The embarrassment broke over my head like a dozen eggs. All my dreams of our 'steadiness' came crashing down. I tried to chuckle too, but my overdone laughter betrayed my defeat. I did not have the skills to recover from a moment like this. I just got up and ran down the stairs and out the door.

My docking mechanism was scorched. I punted the idea of having a girlfriend so far into the future that I couldn't see it. I became a confirmed bachelor, a Peter Pan with no use for growing up, romance, or anything other than goofing off with Gabby. The problem was that this put me on an island by myself. Gabby was free with girls. So were most of the boys I knew. I was the only one locked out for a long time.

I thought about Sheryl for a long time after. I would dream about us holding hands and walking to the TG&Y to buy a soda. She was my first crush. Oh, I would run into her now and then as fall leaves fell outside the stairwell or as the disco ball spun with angst in the Party Room, but it was never the same. That ship had sailed. I would just watch her wistfully from afar and think of what might have been. C'est la vie.

The shell around a boy's heart must be broken for love to grow man-size. Most boys quickly learn to live, risk, and love. I didn't. Without that shell, my choice was to hide my heart from girls. Yet, no matter how hard I tried to ignore the mooing, I just couldn't run the cattle out of town. Girls were here to stay. Still, I managed to avoid serious contact with the fair sex until I was deep into High School. More about that later.

Learning to Sweep

My dad, Larry Lawler (El Jack), was in the
first class of kids to complete four years at
Mira Costa. He was an award winner in
woodshop. His name might still be on the wall
there. He was a consummate craftsman. He
became a floor covering installer and worked throughout the
South Bay, putting in linoleum, carpet, and tile. He used to bring
me along to work as a mule, prepping floors, cleaning up scraps,
and lugging tools. He taught me to sweep a floor so clean you
could eat off it (if you're a dog) by screwing with my mind.
Here's how he did it.

I was about 10-11 years old, and we were on the job at a big
house in the Riviera. It was a very picky customer, so everything
had to be perfect. The floor had to be totally clean, or stuff
would show up through the linoleum. My dad told me to sweep
it. I went to the truck and found a broom. I swept the floor pretty
good (I thought). He came to check on me and saw me standing
there with the broom. He took the broom and broke it over his
thigh and then gave me a little hand broom and told me to sweep
it again on my hands and knees. (I think he only brought that
broom so he could sacrifice it with dramatic effect). Fine. I got
on my hands and knees and swept it again. I was surprised how
much stuff I missed with the big broom. When I was done, he
checked by sweeping it himself. Amazingly, he came up with a
dustpan of stuff I had missed. He told me to sweep it again. I
really bore down on the job this time, determined not to leave a
single speck behind. When he came to check my work, he swept
up yet another dustpan full of stuff. How could this be? He just

said, "This time, sweep it, don't play with it." I attacked that floor, determined to sweep it so hard that it would bleed. When he came to check, he began to sweep it. That's when I saw it. He had a handful of sweepings that he was sprinkling on the floor ahead of him. "Hey! You've got stuff in your hand!" I said. He stopped and looked at me with one eyebrow cocked. Then he dropped the broom and dustpan and ran out of the room. I chased him, and he let me tackle him on the front lawn laughing his ass off.

For a few years, Dad used to work with my Uncle Bud. Uncle Bud didn't set the bar; he WAS the bar my dad could never live up to. El Jack was a touchy and emotional gunslinger, where Uncle Bud was a calm, professional who did his work with perfection. I think Bud Jerand is the only reason my dad had a trade. He mentored him and made sure my dad could provide for us. Uncle Bud was a gem. If you were one of the people who had your floors installed by Black and White Floor Covering, you know what I mean. They were fixtures on Aviation Blvd. just south of Manhattan Beach Blvd for decades.

Uncle Bud also had a son. Steve was a few years older than me, and I kind of idolized him. I didn't really know him that much, but he was a drummer in a band, he dated actual girls, and he knew lots of technical stuff that his dad taught him. That pretty much put stars in my eyes.

One time we had a big job to do that called for all hands on deck. It was a huge job tearing up tiles and replacing them at an oil refinery office. It had to be done after hours over three nights. There was a crew of about ten men. El Jack brought me along, and Uncle Bud brought his son Steve. I was about 11-12 years old, and I think Steve was a sophomore at Aviation HS. Our responsibility was to clean up all the chipped tile and drag the trash cans out to be dumped in the bin. It was hard, filthy work. I was in over my head, but I didn't want to show up like a pussy to Steve, so I kept slogging along.

During this ordeal, Steve was my life raft. He kept my spirits up by telling me jokes and clowning around when Uncle Bud wasn't watching. He had worked under his dad's whip before, and I think he took pity on me. Uncle Bud was from the old school. When you get tired, you don't stop and rest; you just press on until you break through to your 'second wind'. I didn't know I had a second wind. I could barely use up my first wind. That meant the laborers were all supposed to soldier on no matter what. Thanks to Uncle Bud, I know how to do that now. I don't think today's kids know anything about pressing themselves past what they think is their limit.

The third night of the job was brutal. Lack of sleep and what seemed like no end in sight started to take a toll. Steve was wobbling. He knew better than to complain. Being the son of Bud Jerand came with expectations. He began to get in my head. He explained how very valuable our labor was to the job and how little we were being paid. He got me riled up. At the lunch break, about 2 am, I got bold and told my dad Steve and I deserved more money for our part of the job. Steve hid behind a desk and watched to see what would happen.

El Jack and Uncle Bud both broke out laughing for a moment then went quiet. Uncle Bud's eyes were downcast with disappointment. My dad laid it out to me. It went something like this:

"We didn't have to take you on this job. I let you come so you can see how men work. Anyone of these Mexicans here would have loved to take their sons on this job. They would have outworked you both and given all the money they made to their family. What are you going to do with what I pay you? Buy comic books? The best thing you can do right now is shut up and finish this job like your life depended on it."

"That goes for you too, Steve," added Uncle Bud.

You could cut the shame with a knife after that. We finished the work, and I took the cash my dad gave me like it was a snake.

Back in the day, this is how men wrung the child out of their sons. El Jack started the process but left me unfinished when he left our family. Thank God Coach Cooper at Mira Costa finished the job a few years later.

Rockets to the Moon

Gabby and I had a healthy appetite for mayhem and a passionate love for fireworks. The 4th of July was the holiest day of the year for us. The three weeks leading up to it were our Mardi Gras. That was when Red Devil, Freedom, Black Cat, and others would open their firework stands for business. We weren't alone. Every boy our age was lathered up in firework frenzy for most of June. The smell of cordite never left the air around Bay Village.

Everyone knows that Red Devil fireworks were 'Safe and Sane'. Too bad the boys that spent all their money on them weren't. We were all mad scientists when it came to bending fireworks to do our bidding. Crimp a Piccolo Pete 2/3 down the shaft, and it screams a little, explodes a lot. Sparklers are great delayed fuses. Smoke bombs return to school in June like the swallows to San Juan Capistrano. Don't even get me started on Mexican fireworks.

I remember walking down the beach in Hermosa on the Fourth of July in 1967 and dodging firecrackers, bottle rockets, and airborne sparklers. A hazy cloud of smoke hung over the beach at sunset, reddening the failing daylight with joy. All across the sands, small eruptions of cones, piccolos, M80s, firecracker strings, mortar shells, and bottle rockets whipped my lust for mayhem to a fever pitch. As I got a little older, Gabby and I got a little more sophisticated in our misuse of fireworks. It got us in a pickle that we almost didn't get out of.

We had discovered Estes model rockets sometime before. It was fun shooting them off and chasing the parachute drifting rocket down the field. If you were lucky, it didn't get caught in a tree or on a rooftop. Of course, we maxed out the engine size on small rockets and made them fly so high they went completely out of sight. Where did they go? Why, to the Moon, of course. This gave inspiration for us to write a theme song for our rocket daze: (To be sung in 4/4 time as you march)

Ro - ckets, to the Moon! Raww - ketts, to the Mooon!

We will all be go-ing-there soon, in our Raww-kets to the Mooooooon!

Whenever we could scrounge up enough cash to buy an Estes rocket, we would sing this theme with all the drama of Luciano Pavarotti as we marched to the field behind West High with our latest flaming phallic creation. Then our 12-year-old boy brains got struck with zeitgeist one June, and we Yenta-ed a match made in pre-pube hell: Fireworks and Rockets.

First, we bought a good-sized rocket that had big fins below and small dorsal fins halfway up. An artist need a big canvas, right? Then we brought out the Arsenal and went to work. Sparklers attached to each tail fin. Firecrackers mounted with fuses taped to the tail end of each sparkler. Three smoke bombs and an M80 loaded in the fuselage to be ignited by the parachute charge. Four bottle rockets, resting in straw launching tubes glued to each dorsal fin (pylon) with their fuses leading into the fuselage. This sucker was getting heavy. It was a lot for a C-7 engine to lift, so we added eight crimped Piccolo Petes mounted in twos between each fin for added thrust.

(Kids, don't try this at home because you will get caught and sent directly to hell without passing 'Go' or collecting $200. With this warning, I absolve myself of any culpability in what you might do. I wash my hands of any guilt about your doom. You are already dead to me.)

We stood back and admired our work. A moment of silent awe. A name! We must have a name for this chariot of the gods of mayhem. I had an idea. I went and got two glasses of Kool-Aid. Then I proposed a toast. "To the Achievement of a lifetime. May our descendants sing the tale of this day around campfires of the future; the day we spawned..... 'The Kraken.'
We downed our Kool-Aid and shattered the glasses on the concrete. Then we swept up the mess and prepared to unleash our madness on the South Bay.

We marched down Del Amo Blvd. Gabby proudly held our beast, and I carried the launching tower and ignition module. We began humming, then singing our anthem. Quietly at first, like a prayer, then building with intensity until tears filled our eyes. I thought I saw other boys stop and bow their heads as we passed, young mothers squeaked and pulled their babies indoors, and teenage girls dropped their cans of Tab and swooned.
Dogs barked. Cats hissed. All of Torrance and Redondo Beach felt a shudder as if the shadow of a vulture passed over them.

It was late in the day, and twilight roasted the clouds overhead a bright orange against the deep blue. We only had a half-hour or so before darkness would devour the sky. Our first plan was to go to West High's back open field, but a stiff breeze was blowing from the north. We thought it better to set up our launch on the school's front lawn so the breeze would take the Kraken over the school and land it in the open field. The fact that the whole school would be exposed to destruction never entered our lust drunk minds.

Quickly, I assembled the launch pad. I angled the guide rail slightly into the wind, and Gabby mounted the Kraken and connected the electric leads to the ignition wires. I unwound the chord to its full length and stood by. Gabby and I looked at each other one last time, this side of innocence.

"Do we have a closed circuit?" asked Gabby. I inserted the 'key' and pressed down. The indicator light shone bright yellow.
"Closed-circuit confirmed", I said. I released the pressure, and the light relaxed. The ignition wiring was ready for action. We had one chance to get this right. Gabby struck a match. He lit a loose sparkler and used it to light the four sparklers mounted on the fins. When they were all lit, he ran back to me. It was now or never.

"3.. 2.. 1.. ignition!" Gabby commanded. I obeyed by pressing the Key home and lighting the indicator. When it was shining brightly, he barked, "LAUNCH!" I pressed the button...................

Nothing happened at first, and we thought we might have a bad fuse and the Kraken would burn on the pad. Just when hope began to wobble, that mighty C-7 engine roared to life. The rocket began to creep ever so slowly up the guidepost. A regular rocket would go,' Pffft!' and be gone instantly. As powerful as it was, it was evident that the Estes engine was not strong enough to lift the payload. It begged for help. Then the 8 Piccolos began to light up, each one screaming until a chorus of fiery profanity filled the peaceful town of Torrance. The Kraken dragged her heavy ass into the air, belching fire and sparks that looked like the Devil's diarrhea in the twilight.

It was beautiful. A memory that burns in this old man's mind to this day.

Then everything began to get interesting.

The weight of the Kraken exceeded the strength of the launch rail, so it bowed as the rocket left it. The trajectory was skewed due west, about 20 or 30 degrees from vertical. Oh, crap. The firecracker mounted to the sparklers exploded and blew most of the fins off. The Kraken was parallel to the ground, now still under full power but corkscrewing crazy. It cleared the West High grounds. School administrators in their homes inexplicably sighed in relief. The Piccolos reached their crimps and began to blow. Pop! Pop-Pop-Pop, POP! The Estes engine went silent in delay then the parachute charge ignited. This lit the fuse of the bottle rockets, M80, and smoke bombs. The bottle rockets flew off to explode in ecstasy. Then the M80 chimed in. We could just barely see the explosion above the rooftops. Ka-BLAMM. We ran after the Kraken like Dr. Frankenstein chasing his Monster. Where did it go? The smoke bombs gave it away. So did the soft orange glow of a fire. The Kraken had landed in an open drainage pit west of Henrietta (maybe where Sunny Glen Park is now?) I can't remember exactly. We didn't get a good look at the crash site because the sound of sirens met our ears. Then the thought of villagers with pitchforks and torches made us feel like we better turn around and run for our lives.

Well, all is well that ends well. The Fire Department put the blaze out and never found out who started it. Did we learn our lesson? What do you think?

I have suffered from rocket disease ever since. I can't stay away from them, and there is no Rocket-a-holics Anonymous. As a young father, my addiction led me to put on the 4th of July shows for my church in fireworks-free Whittier featuring all kinds of bastardized flying tragedies. I refined a monster called 'The War Wagon', a rocket-propelled Tonka truck festooned with flaming death. It would cap off every year's celebration. After setting one church family's blanket on fire, sticking blazing rockets like arrows in the backyard of many neighbors, and floating lit sparklers on the roofs of houses, I finally got sober. I still love me some rockets, but I lay off the added fireworks. Now I am content to pack my rockets with dollar bills for kids to chase or sometimes dried dog poop to confuse the rabble. There are so many rockets stuck in the trees near my home people think it's some kind of fruit. But I know it's the fruit of two boy's mental illness and one mutha of a beast that once lit the sky of the South Bay on a hot summer evening in '69. The Kraken.

Part 2 - Manhattan Beach

Landing on the Moon

It was 1969, and I was dropping into a comfortable groove. I was a seventh-grader at Grace Wright in Torrance, just owning the school with my best friend, Gabby. I played drums in our band, the 'Twilight Twitchers,' and the Party Room at the Bay Village apartments was our steady gig. I was famous for my rendition of the drum solo from 'Hawaii 50'.

My oldest sister, Margie, was a freshman at West High School. She was at the top of her class, poised to become the Most Popular Girl on campus. Kate, my second oldest sister, still ruled the tetherball courts as an eighth-grader at Grace Wright. She was best friends with my heartthrob Sheryl Weeks. Everyone in my family was settling in except my Dad. El Jack was digging out.

It helps me to remember that my Dad was about thirty-two years old at this point. Remember when you were thirty-two? That is a pretty restless age. El Jack hadn't made his mark on life yet. He was working as a floor covering installer under the shadow of my Uncle Bud, who was established in this trade and successful at just about everything he touched. Uncle Bud owned a house, owned a business, was married to a beautiful, hard-driving wife (my Auntie Pat) had three spectacular kids (Darlene, Sandy, and Steve) who were all doing great in school. Uncle Bud was a rock while my Dad was still rolling. So, while my sisters and I were in a groove, Dad decided to climb out of the rut. One day, he came home a said he had rented a little house in Manhattan Beach, and we were moving.

This news was shattering. How could I know Manhattan Beach was a huge upgrade? I didn't know anything about M.B. except it was far away from Gabby and filled with bleached out surfer dudes. My middle sister Kate was ok with it because this move came at the natural break between Jr. and Senior High School. Kate was always resilient and adaptable, making new friends as easy as baking cookies. But my oldest sister Margie was devastated. She was just wrapping up her freshman year at West High School, where she was a rising star socially and academically. She was set to rule West H.S., but now she would have to transfer to Mira Costa and start at the bottom. She cried, argued, and threatened to run away, but El Jack wasn't watching or caring. He was moving on up to the West Side.

I told Gabby about this tragedy, and he informed me that his family was moving too. They had a chance to house-sit for a year in Palos Verdes while the owners sailed around the world or something. Great. Just when was he going to tell me about it? I could not believe we were busting up the most excellent two-man act since Abbot and Costello, the Smothers Brothers, and Cheech and Chong. Like it or not, the times; they were a'changing.

Moving day came, and we packed up the truck with our avocado green dining set and beat up Sinatra style furniture. I took one last walk around Bay Village, saying goodbye. Goodbye, to the carport locker that became the Lair of the Puberty Brothers, the dirt clod field out back, the Party room where we learned to slow dance with actual girls, and the olive trees that fed Gabby and me ammunition all those long summer days. Goodbye, community Jacuzzi that never stopped sudsing because we never stopped throwing laundry pellets in it. Goodbye, staircase where I made sweet love to Sheryl Weeks... well.. where at least I made sweet like to her... actually where I barely got an arm around her neck before running away, Ok? Can we just move on?

This sudden move was yet another rug pulled out from my young life. After all the instability I grew up in while we lived in Lake View Terrace, I thought we were finally established. I thought we were planted on solid ground in Torrance, building a 'Leave it to Beaver' life that would never change. Now the pillars of Atlantis were caving in, and the Island was sinking. At least El Jack was staying with Mom and us and not ditching us for greener pastures. I had no choice.

From the vast expanse of Anza Blvd, we wedged into a tiny street just over the hill from the beach. The little house we moved to was on Fourth Street, about five houses west of Valley Drive. This was back when there were not so many McMansions around. Our new home started as a little two-bedroom beach getaway that got added on to in a random way until it filled up the lot. The version we got had a family room added on the back connected to the garage with stairs that led to a master bedroom on top of it. My sisters Kate and Margie had the front bedroom.

My little sister Syndie and I had to share the back bedroom where they broke through the wall to add the family room. That made our bedroom more like a fat hallway. My Mom and El Jack were sequestered high above the garage in the Master Bedroom, far from the maddening crowd. Not so far away that we couldn't hear them fight like jackals constantly. Once we were moved in, Mom, my little sister Syndie and El Jack went shopping. Kate ran for the beach, and Margie ran to find the Dark Side.

My first full day alone in the house happened to be the day Neil Armstrong landed on the Moon. The picture of Armstrong stepping on the Moon was so distorted and grainy I tried to move the antenna around to clear it up. No good. I heard him say, "One small step for Man, one giant leap for Mankind." No kidding. I felt the same way. How was I going to survive on this strange beach planet? I went outside and walked over the hill to the ocean. It was Sunday afternoon, and the Strand was busy, even with the Moon landing being shown on T.V. A few girls walked by with bikinis. I started to feel better about Manhattan Beach. A few bronze gods of surf with long bleached out hair and shirtless chiseled bodies walked by. I looked down at my soft belly and began to worry again.

Scarapooch and Drum Solos

1969 was a pivotal year for me. That summer, we became a legit beach family. My two older sisters locked on and found friends right away. I didn't. The pack of guys around my street were all surf rats. Bronzed, wiry, bleached blond Dudes that lived in a closed cult that worshiped the waves. I was still mostly a nerd from the San Fernando Valley. I didn't fit. So I took shelter in two obsessions, my drums, and my dog.

I had a cheap Japanese set of drums that came with me from Bay Village Apartments in Torrance. I set them up in my family room. As you know, all the houses are set close together on 4th, just west of Valley. When I dropped into my rendition of the 'In-A-Gadda-Da-Vida ' solo, I'm sure all the neighbor's for four houses deep could hear me. That's beach life.

There was a surfer kid about my age who lived right next door that was also a drummer. Marc Smoot was his name. I only know that because my oldest sister Margie dated his big brother, Mel. I never actually met him. I never even saw him, except from a great distance. How is that possible? We just lived two different lives, I guess.

Even though Marc and I were from two different worlds and never met face to face, we spoke the common language of drumbeats. I would play in my family room, and he would play in his. I could plainly hear him, and he could hear me. We would trade solos through the walls. I would rip into something for a while, then stop and listen. Then he would answer with a blistering attack, stop, and listen for my reply. We carried on long drumbeat debates this way.

I have no shame in telling you that Marc was a much better drummer than I was. But I could hold my own. I don't know what kind of drums Marc was playing, but I had a little five-piece set like Ringo played. This kind of kit lends itself to Buddy Rich, Steppenwolf, classic Surf style playing. I beat the hell out of my snare. Marc's solos were so rich, dynamic, and complex. I imagined he had a new generation set with a rack of toms and three levels of cymbals. His solos were more Keith Moon and Ginger Baker style. He was inspiring and challenging. I would work on stuff; then, at the right time of day, I would play some and stop to listen. If Marc were there, he would play back and stop. Then we would proceed to trade off our best to each other for an hour or so. The way we signaled the end of a duel was a snare roll with a cymbal splash. We did this off and on throughout the summer. This was the second-closest thing I had to a friend at that time. But my closest friend, the keeper of my heart, was my dog, Scarapooch.

Scarapooch was supposed to be my older sister Margie's dog. Ridiculous name, right? Margie named it after an English aristocrat. I was not too fond of the name, but dogs have a way of drilling right down into my soul. I fell in love with the puppy like no one else in my family. Margie couldn't match my passion, so she abandoned the dog to me. Scarapooch was a female mutt with strong Lab and Retriever lines but smallish in size, like a Beagle. I bonded with her as only a lonely boy can. She went with me everywhere. She was the only one who was so very happy to see me at the end of the day. She was the only one who wanted nothing more than to sit with her soft head on my lap watching the NFL Today on TV. She seemed to be proud of me after trading solos with Smoot through the walls. We were like a team. She watched me play. She would listen to Smoot's solo then cock her head like, 'is that all he can do?' God knows I loved that dog.

One Saturday morning, I took SP- (Scarapooch) for a walk down Valley to the Safeway on the corner of Manhattan Beach Blvd. I kicked a flattened can like a hockey puck as I walked along. SP would chase it some but was mostly annoyed that I gave it more attention than her. Hmpf. Women. After getting a quart of chocolate milk, we took the back way home down Crest Dr. SP was getting irritated about getting hit in the paws with the puck, so I abandoned it. She still acted chippy all the way home, barking at other dogs, and acting skittish. It was good training for me. I'm sure I'm not the only guy that had to put up with attitude from a girlfriend.

I got home to find everyone was gone. That wasn't unusual. My Dad worked and my sisters were out working the beach. Mom was away with my little sister Syndie. Perfect. No one here to share the chocolate milk with or give me crap about playing my drums too loud. I wondered if Smoot was around.

After pouring an obscenely huge glass of chocolate milk (and chugging the rest right from the carton to destroy the evidence), I went into the family room and pulled my drum set out from the corner as Scarapooch watched me. She was hunkered down on her pillow in the corner -NOT wagging her tail- and that was odd. I got all set up and was about to play when I looked

Scarapooch in the eye. Something was off. I left the drums and went to her, but she backed away a little. She curled up in a dog-ball and moaned slightly as I pet her. Then her moans turned to low growls, and her mouth began to foam. What the hell? I talked to her soothingly, but she wasn't responding to affection. She was getting mad. She was clearly in trouble, but I didn't know what to do. I called my Dad's office, but he was on a job somewhere. I called my mom, who was at my Auntie Pat's house. I told her something was wrong with Scarapooch. At first, she just tried to dismiss me by saying it will be alright. I convinced her it was NOT alright, that SP was growling at me and foaming at the mouth. She said she would be there in 15 minutes. She took over an hour.

In the space of that time, Scarapooch went from sad to suffering to aggressive. It was wrenching to watch this happen with no one there to help. I was just about to go next door to see if Smoot was there when mom came in the door. By that time, Scarapooch was backed up in the family room, ready to attack. The sweet dog I loved was gone. A mad killer was in her place. Her muzzle was completely foamed in. Mom called the police. They sent animal control. They arrived and captured Scarapooch somehow and took her away. On the way out, they said the word 'distemper.' Just like that, she was ripped out of my life. Mom was distracted by having to get back to Auntie Pat's house. I didn't understand then, but now I know she was probably trying to convince her cousin to bail us out again with cash. She hurriedly hugged me and said she would get me another dog and then went back to my aunt's house. No one could see the ragged hole in my heart.

I was alone in the house. I couldn't take my eyes off her pillow and slobbery ball and chewed up slipper that marked the spot where my best girlfriend used to live. Oh, My God, how fast life can change. A boy in love in the morning, a boy utterly alone in the afternoon.

- Drums kicked up next door. Smoot was great, as usual. He stopped and waited for an answer. I sat down behind my drums and forced myself to play. I played for Scarapooch. I played slowly to 'When a Man Loves a Woman' in my mind. No solo, just keeping the beat and trying to keep my eyes clear. I finished with a slow roll on the snare and a soft cymbal crash. After all the commotion with the police and animal control people here, Marc must have sensed something was up. He just answered with a snare roll that slowed to a stop. -

I bawled like a baby for hours. That was my first Great Loss. Life went on. I healed over time. Marc and I still traded solos. I never did meet him face to face. Two years later (over my broken heart objections), we got another dog. Of course, it drilled right into me like I knew it would. My sister named it Oglethorpe. Go figure.

Other things that grew up in Manhattan and Hermosa...

It was the end of a perfect fall day. I had been bodysurfing off Fourth Street all afternoon. I took a hot shower to rinse the salt out and curled up on the sofa with a half bucket of cold KFC while I watched 'This Week in the NFL'. My sister's room was closed, and Led Zeppelin's 'Whole Lotta Love' pounded through the door. I thought that was the dirtiest thing I ever heard, but I loved it. My mom was working on a craft with my little sister, and my dad had just come home from work.

I heard something: a ticking or clicking sound. I tried to ignore it as I watched Roman Gabriel get sacked in slow motion. It was persistent. The clickity sound cut through John Facenda's deep baritone narration of Les Josephson's touchdown run and the muted Zeppelin and when my little sister asked, 'What's that noise?" From the den, I had to get up and find out.

"Mom, what's that noise?" I asked.
"Probably your sisters are doing something."
"It's not coming from their room."
"Then it's your father."
"Dad's in the bathroom."
"Hmm... You're right. What is that?"
"What's that noise?" asked my dad, closing the bathroom door behind him.

I had my sister turn off the stereo, and we could all hear it plainly. It sounded like someone playing with chopsticks. In silence, we all crept through the house, trying to home in on it. We ended up in the kitchen, right over the stove. It was coming from the vent above the burners. The stove wasn't on, so my dad got a screwdriver and took the screws out that held the vent cover on. As soon as the cover was off, out dropped a nightmare.

We all screamed. It was the hugest, nastiest, weirdest looking bug I ever saw. It looked like something from the Outer Limits. Like a giant 'Cooties' bug come to life. It was a four-inch-long Potato Bug, otherwise known as a Jerusalem Cricket. Even my dad, El Jack, the tough son of an Idaho farmer, had a spasm of heebie-geebies that turned our screams into gut-busting laughter. He denied it, saying he was trying to scare it to protect his family. Nice try. We never let him live it down. He picked it up with BBQ tongs, and we all took it out to the yard and set it on the grass where it crept away. This marked one of the few high watermarks of my family life. I never could figure out how a big thing like that could get in there....

And then there were snails...

When I lived on 4th street in Manhattan, our house was one of those tiny two-bedroom cottages that got added-on until it nearly filled the whole lot. We had a little inner courtyard about the size of a bricked bedroom and had a bbq. It was nice, but just patio furniture and potted plants there. We also had a small front yard with grass. That back patio and the front 'lawn' became my responsibility.

My dad tried to teach me about the rewards of work, so he made me earn my $2 allowance by cleaning and watering the back patio plants and cutting the front grass every week. I had other inside chores, but I took some pride in how the front of our house looked.

The first thing I would do was 'work the back forty' (square feet). The courtyard was home to some rotting wood patio furniture and a rusty built-in bbq. Funny, we NEVER went out there. It became the playground for my dog Scarapooch. Picking up dog poop was part of the job. Then I would tend to the back plants. I didn't know their names, and I wasn't very 'green-thumbed' about them, but it was easy enough to water them and pull out the dead stuff. A few passes with a broom, and the little courtyard looked ready for nothing again. I hope Scarapooch appreciated it.

Next was the front' yard'. We had a little push lawnmower, and it only took a few passes to do the whole thing. There were some plants around the front porch to tend, but that was about it. The main problem with the front yard was snails. They were everywhere. They ate the plants and had to be picked up before mowing the lawn. I would search the yard like a kid looking for slimy Easter eggs and round them up in a garbage pail and throw them in the trash. Of course, looking for them meant you encountered the occasional lizard, garden snake, or freakish Potato Bug. All horrors. This nightmare roundup had to be done every week before I could mow. Next week the damn yard was full of them again. This pissed me off.

One week I decided to drop the hammer. I was going to turn the tables on the livestock and become their worst nightmare. I went searching for snails and collected about thirty or so. Instead of throwing them away, I put them in a pile on the grass. Then I stood with my push mower and thought something like, "Today shall be a day of infamy. Woe to the snail that dares slime this yard". I pushed with all my might.

The power shower of snail guts that sprayed up covered the whole front side of my body. It dripped from my hair and even got into my mouth. For a second, I thought, "What the fu..." but then the heebie-jeebies took over, and I convulsed uncontrollably like a baby tasting a lemon. I walked to the back patio where even Scarapooch wouldn't come near me and stripped down to my underwear. I threw my snail soaked shirt and shorts in the trash. Then I remembered that I had locked the back patio door. I banged on the glass, and my little sister Syndie came to the rescue. She didn't open the door; instead, she ran back inside and brought my older sisters out to laugh at me. They wouldn't let me in. I had to go out to the front door, but they locked that one too. This lockout went on for a while until Syndie finally let me in.

They all had a great laugh on me. They were so busy having a good time; they didn't notice the snails I put under their bedsheets.

The Siren of 4th Street

When I lived in Lake View Terrace as a little kid, we only went to an actual beach maybe three times in my first ten years. That happened on the rare occasion that we visited Grandmother Fergie in N. Redondo Beach. She lived in the neighborhood just north of Artesia and about a half-mile west of Hawthorne, across the street from an elementary school on Ruhland. My Uncle Bud and Auntie Pat lived near Aviation High School, and they had teenagers just a little older than us. I vaguely remember being taken to Hermosa Beach in the oldest cousin's car. I had to be only 6 or 7 years old. The only thing I remember about that day was that the teenage daughters never went in the water. They didn't throw a frisbee, whack a paddle ball or toss a football on the sand. They just laid on the sand as still as death and cooked. They were 'working on their tan.' I didn't get it. Why would you come to the beach and just lay there?

Years later, when we had moved to Manhattan, I had a better grasp of the idea. Having brown skin was 'in.' I guess it proved you were at the beach. Okay, now I bet there is a lot of my generation who wished they worked less on their tan and more on avoiding melanoma. Anyway, as a young teenager, I finally understood the lying on the beach thing. I also understood why tourists that don't live at the beach are so busy trying to wring every last drop of activity out of their precious day trip.

About a week after we moved into our small cottage on 4th street, I walked down to the Strand and out on the sand. It was a Wednesday morning, so there weren't many people around. I threw my towel down and laid it out on the sand, just like a local. I noticed that when you get your head right down to the sand, the sound changes. You can hear things way down the beach. I could hear music drifting along from somewhere, people talking on the Strand, and the muffled sound of the breakers hitting the shore. Very peaceful.

While I lay there 'working on my tan,' my attention was drawn to another guy lying on the beach about a hundred feet away. My perspective was an inch off the deck with my head sideways. Something was... off about this guy. I saw a couple of other dudes about the same distance away on the other side who were sitting up looking at this odd guy. I picked myself up on one elbow and was startled. This was no guy; it was a topless girl lying there getting a tan where the sun don't normally shine. Heavens to Mergatroid, I'm not in Kansas anymore.

This vision rattled around in my head. It was too confounded to percolate downward and register with my junior brain. I didn't stare; I just lay there looking now and then while trying to keep my cool. I don't remember if she was attractive or what color her hair was because I couldn't take my eyes off the prize. There they are, right out in the open. I've seen photos but here was a real girl! Incredible. I kept waiting for my engine to fire up, but there was no context for this revelation. There was no relationship with this girl to give her action any meaning. The whole experience was strangely academic. The dudes on the far side thought differently. They decided to make a move.

I could hear clearly everything they said, but I don't remember much. One guy just got up and casually walked over and said something like, "Hey girl. I thought the least I could do is come over and say hi." She didn't respond to him other than pull on a bikini top and gather her things and walk off the beach. The show was over. Even though he got shot down, he strutted like a rooster walking back to his friend, and they laughed like jackals.

What is this place? There must be something about the sand that makes people crazy. I thought about this for a long time, laying there working on my sunburn. Of course! The beach is the edge of the wilderness. On the inland side of the shore, the constraints, troubles, complications, and governments of civilization work to domesticate the human animal. Yet, on the wet side of the sand, the forces of elemental nature rule. When a boy or girl feels the sand between their toes, the primal ocean pulls a tide of something ancient up to the surface. The civilized part is left on the bottom like ballast in a ship. When an ocean breeze catches hold of that wild thing inside, all possibilities set sail. This, more than anything else, I think, is what binds us together as a tribe. No matter where we stray across the wide Earth, the sound of surf will always be a siren song, a battle anthem, and a lullaby all at once.

When I finally walked home that day, I was a wiser boy. I paid for my wisdom with a branded image of a topples girl on my brain that troubled me for a long time and a sunburn so hot it could roast marshmallows.

MB Blues

The first summer Saturday I lived in Manhattan Beach, I woke up with way too much time on my hands. I knew I was supposed to be in paradise. The blue waves and shimmering sands were just a few blocks away. Countless girls in bikinis were strolling along the Strand. The coastal overcast was just beginning to burn off, and the Beach Boys were on the radio. Dad was off at work, Mom was sleeping in the back master bedroom, and my older sisters were in their room, still snoring deep in their 'beauty sleep.' That left me and my little sister, Syndie, alone to find something to do.

I was twelve; she was 7. Syndie was the cutest little curly hair blonde in her onesy. She was my little buddy. Through all the turmoil of moving around, enduring my parent's fighting, Syndie clung to me. She called me 'Ga-Ga.' I took big-brothering seriously. I did my best to clown around with her and make her childhood as fun as I could. I made up a make-believe friend for her with my fingers called 'Little Friend.' I would walk my hand around using my middle and ring finger for legs and my first and pinky for arms. There was no head, but that didn't stop Syndie from falling in love with Little Friend. Little Friend had a dog named 'Doggy' (my creativity was just lazy back then). Doggy was my other hand, walking on fingers with my middle finger as its' head.'

Syndie shared a bedroom with me, so we would generally wake up together. We would lie awake in our beds on opposite walls making fart sounds to each other and pretending to fling boogers at each other; you know, 'brother' stuff. Then I would get out of bed, kneel beside her bed and walk Little Friend over to see if she wanted to play.

"Excuse me, is Tinny home?" Little Friend would ask.

"I'm right here, silly." she would answer. (She would speak to Little Friend, completely ignoring me).

"Have you seen Doggy? I lost him." (crying)

"Aww, don't cry; I'll help you find Doggy. Here, Doggy Doggy!"

My other hand would appear from behind my back with Doggy jumping and running around. Little Friend would be soo happy.

"Thank you, Tinny. There's Doggy Boy. (I would crank my fingers to make Little Friend hug and stroke Doggy as realistically as I could.) Syndie would pet Doggy and pretend to give him food.

Suddenly, Doggy would yelp and whimper and run away behind my back.

"What's the matter, Doggy?" Asked Syndie.

"He's scared. He must hear something," said Little Friend. "Listen!"

"Rawwwer! Where is he?" I say, in a wicked voice.

"It's the Monster! says Little Friend. He shivers and runs to Syndie.

"Don't be scared. I'll protect you."

"Look out! There he is!" says Little Friend. My other hand comes crawling in sight, like a giant spider.

"Where is that sniveling punk, Little Friend?" says the Monster. "Oh, there you are! Rawwwer! You can't hide from me! I'm going to bite your legs off!"

The Monster makes a move for Little Friend, and Syndie screams, "NO!" She slams down on my 'Monster' hand and cranks all my fingers back till they are almost breaking. Oh, my God, It hurts so bad, but it's so funny how ferocious she gets; I'm laughing through my tears. Little Friend goads her on.

"Get him! Beat him up, Tinny!" Syndie does her best to destroy my other hand until I have to make it drag away, moaning, and hide behind my back. Then, (amazingly), Doggy comes back! Little Friend and Doggy come close and give her a big hug between my first and fourth fingers. Syndie just loves this. She would do this every day. She is the undisputed Champion of Little Friend and Doggy.

Well, that burns the first hour or so of the morning. Soon, Mom wakes up and takes Syndie with her to Del Amo Mall. My older sisters get up and realize the beauty sleep didn't work, so they spend an hour desperately primping themselves and then leave to find their boyfriends. I'm left alone in the house. I play a drum solo on my kit and wait to see if Marc Smoot (the drummer kid I never met who lives next door) plays one back, but I get crickets. He must be out surfing or something. By now, the sun is full blast. I pull on my Levi cut-offs, white t-shirt, and beat up PF Flyers (no socks) and grab a towel, and out the door, I go.

I was between bikes at that point. My Stingray was stolen, and my Mom hadn't bought me my Schwinn Varsity yet, so I was on foot. No problem. I found an empty Coke can and flattened it with a stomp of my foot. I kicked this puck ahead of me as I went along. I made these anytime I had to walk a long way. They were slightly amusing but not so distracting that you would get hit by a car or something. They helped me think. They gave me just enough canvass to paint whatever was on my mind as I walked along. I call these things a 'kickit.'

(Just a side note. I think someone should market Kickits, maybe a hacky-sack like thing made of natural jute and filled with grass seed or bark so if you lost it, the thing would dissolve naturally. Maybe more kids would use their legs instead of gliding around on hoverboards. I laugh when I see those things. Impressive technology, right? But seriously, it's like they are saying, "I refuse to use these annoying meat sticks that hang off my butt! I'm done with them!". At least we had to push our skateboard now and then. What are your legs for? I say, "use 'em or lose 'em").

That summer day in '68 wasn't too hot, but the sun-blessed the landscape with every color. The air was almost wet with cool, clean freshness, scented with salt from the ocean. This was normal for MB but was foreign to me. I was used to heat and smog from living in Torrance and Lake View Terrace before that. I don't trust air that clean. You can't even see it. How do you know it's there?

I smacked my kickit west towards the beach and then north on Manhattan Ave. Pretty soon, the cottages gave way to the retail area. Back then, MB was just mom and pop stores, no high-end glamor franchises yet. Man, has that ship sailed or what?

I knew there was a toy store along the way, near downtown. I had seen it but never been in it, and I was always a sucker for toy stores ever since I was a kid. Of course, It wasn't the kind of place that sold the violent, destructive toys I favored. You wouldn't find a 'Johnny 7' military gun or a Man From U.N.C.L.E. Attaché case with ten weapons built-in. This store was genteel. I can't remember its name, but I want to say, Manhattan Toy and Variety? It was the kind of toy store that Geppetto might own. It had nice toys that I thought my little sister might like. I had a few bucks. I thought about getting her something from Little Friend.

I wandered around looking for the right toy. Syndie wasn't too much into baby dolls. Thank God, I didn't want to have to be seen buying a baby doll. A 12-year-old can only stand so much pressure on my self-image. It came down to a little guy made from wooden beads that collapsed when you pushed the bottom of his stand in or a guy suspended by a wooden stick that would tap dance when you tapped on the stick. I went with the collapsing dude—only $2 and more comfortable to carry in my back pocket. Also, I thought he might make a good punching bag for Little Friend.

Back on the street, I walked to MB Blvd. and down to the pier. The Strand was pretty busy that day. The sun was getting warm, and there were many local guys around with no shirts on. I noticed a similarity. They all had these arms like apes, big pecks, and A-frame traps, but they were still ten-year-olds from the chest down. Then I figured it out. It was from endless paddling on surfboards. Their legs were only good for standing on surfboards, but the upper body did all the work. That body type (topped off with long bleached hair) was a race of humans only found near the coast. I was not of that race. My shirt was staying on, hiding my white skin and soft belly. But nothing was covering my eyes. They were getting peeled by all the beautiful girls in bikinis that were everywhere. Brother, I'm not in Kansas anymore.

I walked down the steep grade of Manhattan Beach Blvd to the Strand and had a choice to make. Go out on the pier and check out the fishing, or turn south and cruise the Strand. Hmm... Fishing is ok; I like to see what's being caught, peer down into the clear waters and watch the surfers ride the rollers. But seriously, what choice did I have? Whoever invented the idea of girls walking around wearing basically colorful underwear in public is either a genius or a madman. I don't know if I want to buy him a cigar or punch him in the nose. Nothing delighted me and caused me more trouble than the feast for the eyes laid out in the sun every day in MB. I took the Strand.

No sooner had I turned south, the strains of the Beach Boys song, 'Girls on the Beach', came on someone's radio. Take a second and listen to it on YouTube. https://youtu.be/s4EhPwBKHkQ You will understand why I felt I had accidentally stepped into a promotional shoot for South Bay beach life. Those velvet harmonies made the Strand seem like the buffet at Caesar's Palace. I lingered in range of the music and tried to let Brian Wilson teach me something. He promised that 'the girls on the beach are all within reach...' Ok, sounds good; sign me up. But then the critical bit of the song kicks in, '... IF you know what to do'. That's where I came up empty. I had no clue. I was not of this race. MB boys had the sun-bleached looks of Aquaman. I looked like Acne-man. They cruised along the Strand like a little Duce Coupe. I waddled along like a Winnebago. They had the confidence of a Great White. I flopped along like a harbor seal. But, hey, I'm only 12, I can learn, right?

I walked down the Strand to 4th street where I lived, but instead of going home, I needed to hit the surf and burn off some of the high octane hormones that were making me sick by then. The sun was pretty hot. I was glad I had my shoes, or the sand would have fried my feet. I got down to the shore and threw my towel down, and pulled off my shoes. Then I hesitated and looked around. I expected to see everyone watching me for the big reveal when I pulled my t-shirt off. God, I hated that moment. I used to see these Mexican guys that would go in the surf with their jeans and T-shirts on and wonder if they had it right. No... I knew if I ever went 'foreigner' and went in the water fully clothed, I would never go back. So I braced my mind and pulled the shirt off. No one screamed, babies didn't weep, no one tried to push me back in the surf. No one cared. But just in case, I ran and jumped into the surf.

The water was crystal clear that day. The surf wasn't huge, but it was muscular. Surfers were out past the shore break, riding tight green tubes. I went out about as far as I could while keeping in touch with the sand bottom. I didn't know much about body surfing, so I just flailed when any wave came along. The wave would pick me up and leave me behind, laughing as it broke. I did this for a while when I attracted the attention of an old guy with a beard who was body surfing next to me. He watched me throw myself at every lump of water like an ugly hooker trying to snag drunk sailors at the Pike.

"Slow down, brah," he said," If the wave ain't pulling you, it don't want you."
"What do you mean?" I asked.
"Put your feet on the sand and feel for the power. A lot of these waves are just sidekicks for the real breakers. They have no suck. They are 'Panchos'. Wait for 'Cisco'."

As he explained this, a few weak waves passed us, and he waved them off. Then one came that sucked so hard it almost pulled me off my feet. The man turned and timed it and launched easily into it and rode it almost all the way in.

"That was a Cisco. See?"
"I think so."
"Now, you do it. Just watch out for surfers riding in. They will slice you up like deli meat if you get in their way."

Soon I felt a wave pulling me. It was going to break just past me, so I launched into it, and it shot me down the face with my head out of the water at terrific speed. It was exhilarating. I was hooked. The old guy gave me a thumb and pinky 'Bonaroo' sign and left me to my honeymoon. I rode all afternoon until I was exhausted.

When I finally dragged out of the water and flopped on my towel, I was at peace with the world. For the first time, I felt that I owned this beach life a little, and it owned me too. I walked back up Fourth Street to my house. Suddenly, I remembered that I forgot about the little collapsing bead man I bought for my little sister that I had in my pocket. He was gone. Oh, well. He's probably still out there riding the surf off Fourth Street, Manhattan Beach. Cowabunga, little dude....

The Ghost in my Shorts

Remember OP shorts? I didn't have those. When I was thirteen, I wore cut-off jeans for shorts back then. Cut-off jeans and a plain white t-shirt with PF Flyers on my feet were my basic uniform when I lived in Lake View Terrace. I imported this North San Fernando Valley fashion statement to the South Bay, but it didn't stick. Turns out that the South Bay had its own ideas about how they would dress when they 'just didn't care what they looked like.' 'Surf Bum' was the standard. Years later, a little tear came to my eye when I saw "The Sandlot," a movie set in the N. San Fernando Valley featuring the kind of scruffy kids that I played with. We rocked the 'refugee urchin' look.

So I had this one pair of cut-off Levi's for more than a year. They started out about mid-thigh length, but the raw-cut edge would unravel and get ragged and stringy. It needed periodic 'hair cuts' to keep the fringe under control. With every trim, the shorts got a little shorter. When a pair of these got so short they qualified as 'Daisy Dukes,' it was time to chuck 'um (or cross over and bat for the other side).

I was wearing my favorite cut-offs one late afternoon when I went to the beach. I swam, and body surfed all day off 4th Street. The ocean was different that day. Kinda stinky, and the water wasn't clear like it usually was. It didn't put me off. By this time, I had experienced many versions of surf. Sometimes the surf was choked with so much seaweed it was creepy to swim in. Other times, it was so clear, you could see the bottom for twenty feet in all directions. The occasional jellyfish invasion made swimming dicey. Sometimes tar would drift in from the oil tankers waiting to hookup at the refinery intake, just offshore at El Porto. Black stains would stick to your feet for days after. I just took it as it came.

This day, not too many people were in the water. In fact, no one was in the water. That wasn't going to stop me. When I began to step into the surf, an old sun-baked Mexican guy walking along the beach said,

"You sure you want to do that? It's a red tide today."
I didn't want to appear stupid, so I answered,

"The fish swim in it, good enough for me."

"The feesh die in it." He pointed to a small dead fish tangled in some seaweed.

"I'm bigger than a fish," was my snappy retort as I dived into a wave. I came up and shook the water out of my hair. I heard the man say, "Via con Dios," as he walked on. See how not-stupid I was?

I body surfed for more than an hour or so until I got weirded out by all the junk swirling in the filthy water. It kept hitting me and trying to find a way into my mouth. The sun had set, and the crazy pink-orange Picasso sky was burning overhead. Finally, I gave up and hiked back up the hill and over to home near Valley View.

When I got back, my Mom caught a whiff of me and said, "You stink, Honey. Go take a shower before I have to bury you in the backyard." I didn't smell anything, but by that time, I was nose blind. So I pulled off my shorts and, like any young teenager, left them right where they dropped in the middle of my bedroom floor. I showered the saltwater off and felt soft as a baby's butt. Mom had hamburger steaks, rice, and canned green beans ready for dinner. That's what we call a Lake View Terrace Feast, so I dug in. A pound of meat later, I crowded next to Syndie on the sofa, and we watched "13 Ghosts" on Chiller TV. She fell asleep next to me, so I helped put her to bed, and I crawled under my covers on the other side of the room and was out in seconds.

It was pitch black when I woke up having to pee. I had a series of dreams about going pee but kept coming to consciousness with my problem still there. I became afraid that the next dream would open the flood gates and soak my bed, so I crawled out of a dead sleep. It knew which way the bathroom was, even in the dark, so I stepped in that direction. My foot hit something wet.

This was shocking by itself because I didn't expect it, but when the room lit up with a creepy green light, my heart jumped in my throat. I looked down and saw my cut-off Levi's glowing with what I could only imagine was the misery of the un-dead. Here in my own room, a Ghost had possessed my shorts. This reality, where Satan had opened a gateway from the bowels of Hell into the world of Men through my shorts, only lasted about ten seconds, but it seemed like a terrifying eternity. Here was the '14th Ghost'.

It's amazing that I didn't lose it right there and drown my room with a fire hose. But I didn't. God threw me a bone. "Red Tide" is all I heard in my head. With that tip, the schemes of the devil unraveled like the fringe of my cut-offs, and peace was restored. I went to the bathroom, took care of business, and then returned to kick my shorts a few more times for fun. Each time, the glow got fainter. I thought about waking up my little sister, but she was dug in and drooling on her pillow. I went back to bed.

The next evening, I took Syndie down to the beach after the sun had set, and we watched the microbiology miracle light up the waves in a magical glow. It was delightful, then cool, then boring. We walked back home and didn't pay any more attention to the Red Tide. Just one of those fantastic things you can take for granted when you live at the beach. You know what I mean.

A Man and his Horse

I know it's hard to believe, but there was a time when kids knew little to nothing about skateboards. They existed, but in the form of short planks with steel skate wheels attached. You could go in a straight line, but God forbid you touch a pebble; you would fly ass over elbows and acquaint yourself with the sidewalk. It wasn't until Frank Nasworthy put polyurethane wheels on decks that skateboarding took off. Even then, the revelation was mostly a Beach Cities thing that most inland kids didn't know about yet. Back then, in my kingdom on Anza in Torrance, if a kid needed to get around, it was on a Stingray bike.

When I lived at the Bay Village Apartments, I got a genuine blue Schwinn Stingray for my 11th birthday. I owned and cherished that treasure- for about a month. That's how long it took for someone to steal it. After it was gone, my mom bought a faded blue Huffy stingray knock off from a yard sale to replace it. It was bent and rusted enough to make it safe from thieves. Even though I kept a sharp eye out for my beautiful blue stallion, I never saw it again. Slowly I got over the loss and bonded to the Huffy. It had the same banana seat and ape-hanger grips inspired by the choppers from Easy Rider. This old steed served me well on the flatlands of Torrance. I delivered my paper route with this bike with the big canvass bags filled with the Herald Examiner swinging from the handlebars. I rode countless trips south down Anza to the TG&Y by Torrance Blvd or north to the liquor store at Del Amo, where I bought my comic books. My friends and I would ride like a pack of wolves around the West High school campus in the summer playing bike tag. Some guys even weaponized the handlebars by spanning the gap with rubber bands to fire bobby pins with the velocity of a bullet. That was not my thing, and we avoided those hooligans. Instead, Gabby and our crew would spend dusty-dirty hours jumping rickety ramps in the dirt lot behind my apartments. We were off-road way before Mountain Bikes became a thing. My trusty, 'Ding-ray' never failed me. That beat-up bike extended my preteen footprint to about ten-fifteen blocks in every direction. Given the concentration of kids that lived in those apartments on Anza, that was more than enough.

When my family moved from Anza in Torrance to 4th Street, Manhattan Beach, I still had the single gear Ding-ray with its banana seat and high handlebars. After the move, I soon found out that it wasn't as well suited for the hilly beach towns. It was a breeze gliding downhill to the strand but a bitch grinding back uphill to go home. I didn't suffer long because two weeks after I moved there, it was also stolen. It broke my heart to lose my old friend. Without my wheels, I was reduced to creeping around the streets on foot like a mangy, (ugh) pedestrian. I needed a bike, but not just any bike. I needed an upgrade in technology. It came in the form of an old Schwinn Varsity 10 speed.

My mom found this old battle-ax at another yard sale and bought it for $15. It wasn't sexy, it wasn't impressive, and it wasn't built for speed. It was made to be punished. The frame was as heavy as a Buick and the curled under handlebars reminded me of Bighorn sheep. But I was grateful, and I poured love into this Orc and transformed it into an Elfish Warhorse. I took the tires off and steel-wooled the rims until they shined like Mithril. I rewrapped the handlebars with the hide of the wild Drake (duct tape). I repainted the frame a deep blue using cobalt dug from the great Dwarf Clan of Rustoleum's mines. After I had reassembled it and lubricated its gears with oil from the head of the 3 in 1 Kraken, it was ready. I bought a heavy chain bike lock and scored the combination on my skull. Now I was ready for adventure.

A name! A legendary name for such a chariot was needed! I whispered to it in the moonlight, "Tell me your name, thou two-wheeled mercurial engine of swift passage, and I will sing songs of your exploits around the campfires of the tribe for generations to come." Several names came to mind as I broke the bike in around Manhattan Beach. 'Crotchgrinder', 'Backbender', 'Pants-leg-snagger'.. all salty and truthful names, yet they all fell to the floor of unworthiness. Then I saw it. Nay, it was before mine eyes all this time! 'Varsity'... So let it be recorded in the Book òf the Elders.

I rode the hell out of Varsity. It took me all the way back to Torrance to see my compadre, Gabby. It took me beyond the bend of Palos Verdes to the gates of Marineland. It took me deep into the inland empire of Hawthorne and Inglewood. It kept me in range of the beach after we had moved to a house east of Aviation Blvd. I installed peddle stirrups that wrapped around my toe to double the power of my stroke. Coming back and forth over the hills had built my leg strength to the point I could grind straight up the 2nd street hill east of Valley using the highest gear.

One particular day, after body surfing all afternoon, I forked my bronco and headed east on 2nd Street. I was feeling cocky as a cat with a rat. After I topped the crest at Sepulveda heading east, I powered down the steep backside of 2nd as fast as I could, tucked in like a jockey on Secretariat. As I approached the stop sign at Meadows, I hit a bump, and my front wheel came off. The fork dug in and pitched me over the handlebars. I hit the pavement and rolled like Evel Knievel at Caesar's Palace. After I came to a stop, I lay there thinking about the future. Amazingly, I had no broken bones, only road rash to mark the occasion. The Varsity wasn't damaged at all. I found the wheel and put it back on, and rode the rest of the way home. This bike made a habit of pitching me to the pavement whenever I got a bit full of myself. I never got too hurt; I just bounced like Gumby. I would cuss out that damned thing and get back on. Then an incident happened that made me think about getting a car.

I was riding down PCH past the IHOP that used to be near Pier Ave in Hermosa. I was making pretty good speed when suddenly a parked car threw open their driver's side door right in front of me. Of course, I plowed straight into it and flew over. I hit the ground and rolled a bit into traffic under a bobtail truck that was driving alongside. Time slowed to a crawl. I was laid out between the front and back wheels perpendicular to the truck. The double back wheels were bearing down towards me. I jerked up in a fetal position, and the momentum turned me clockwise so that the tires just grazed my back as they passed. The truck rolled over the Varsity and screeched to a stop. The poor driver came running around, thinking he had rolled over me. He was expecting to see me squished on the road. I only had a torn shirt and a tale to tell (that has grown in detail as the years have passed). The man gave me $100 for my trouble and hightailed it out of there. Incredibly, that immortal Varsity survived. It had a bent wheel, and the handlebars were cockeyed, but I limped it home, replaced the wheel, and rode it for years.

I loved-hated that bike, even though it tried to kill me several times. I rode it all through High School and into my early years of work as a bus driver. Even after I bought my first car (a '57 Ford Fairlane), I kept it. The damn Ford hardly ever ran, so the bike was still numero uno. Finally, we broke up when I fell for a pale green '65 Mustang GT. Gabby sold it to me for $300 and the Varsity a few months before entering the Air Force. With a deep sigh and a rejoicing crotch, I let that Varsity fade into the misty realm of Legend.

Camping Day

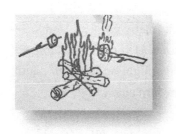

Even though I consider him a South Bay native, my Dad, Larry 'El Jack' Lawler, was born and weaned in Idaho. Remember that barefoot kid in ragged cutoffs that played the banjo in the movie 'Deliverance'? That was my Dad as a kid, minus the banjo. He was only slightly more civilized than a possum. Little Larry and his kid brother Johnny had almost no supervision because his Dad was mostly a no-show truck driver. Late in his life, my Dad revealed just how tragic his upbringing was when he told me about the last time he saw his own father.

He and Johnny were walking barefoot on a remote dirt road in the woods when a truck came up from behind them. They got off the road and saw it was their father driving, so they yelled and waved him down. The truck reluctantly pulled over, and their daddy got out. The brothers hadn't seen him in about a month. That wasn't unusual, given he was a long haul truck driver. The two boys ran to him and gave their daddy a big hug, and asked if they could ride along with him. He said no, that he was doing a delivery in town. He said he would meet them afterward at the drug store and get them an ice cream float. He hugged them, tussled their hair, and drove on.

The two barefoot boys ran the rest of the way into town and pulled up at the drugstore out of breath. They went in and sat at the counter and waited. And waited. Drunk on hope, they waited until it began to get dark, but Daddy didn't show up. Larry sobered up and knew he wasn't going to show, but little Johnny still wanted to keep waiting. When it finally got dark, and the drug store began to close, Johnny cried. He only agreed to go home when Larry told him that daddy might be there. Of course, you know he wasn't. They never saw him again.

When my Dad told me this story, I was almost 60 years old, and El Jack was a fossil circling the drain. Man, did it explain a lot! He never wanted to share this with me before because he thought it would make him seem pathetic. Instead, the old coot rose ten notches on the Hero scale in my eyes. He was a survivor. The way he cared for his little brother, the way he tried to make my childhood stable (in comparison to his), the way he tried to love my alcoholic mother, all while limping around with this gaping wound in his past. Suddenly, all his flaws and failings were reframed in a new context.

This back story explained one of my most fearful episodes of being a boy under El Jack's shadow.

When they were runts, Larry and Johnny ran wild in the woods like animals. As an Idaho kid, being in the outdoors was second nature. When he moved to So Cal, it must have driven him nuts to be so crowded in by people, in a land of mostly pavement. Now and then, the kettle would begin to whistle. El Jack had to get his 'mountain man' on. So we went camping.

Camping was always a rustic adventure with El Jack. He brought along only the bare necessities and loved to 'live off the land.' My mom was the only thing that kept us from having to eat bugs and wear beaver skins. Nevertheless, El Jack made love to the wilderness like a sailor on shore leave. My big sisters and I were

10, 11, and 12, and my little sister Syndie was 5. While Syndie got to stay safe with Mom, Kate, Margie, and I had to run with the Big Possum and keep up. Hell, at ten years old, Larry had skinned a virgin and made love to a cougar, or something like that. That's what he would have us believe. So when he decided to take us older kids on a hike, I feared for my life.

I tried to hide. I had brought a bunch of comic books with me. My plan was to find a cave or a rotten log to hole up in and read about Batman and Green Lantern until the ordeal was over. While El Jack was gearing up for his expedition (pulling a t-shirt over Levi's and lacing up work shoes), I quietly slunk away to my hideout. I could hear him mustering my sisters for duty and asking where I had got off to. Mom wasn't sayin' nuttin. She had sympathy for her little soft blubber boy and tried to make him forget me. Good 'ol Mom, she always had my back. It didn't work. He was determined to hatch the larva and bring forth a man in me. He looked around, examined a bendy blade of grass, a scuff on a rock, and zeroed in on my Fortress of Solitude. As he yanked me out of my hole, I asked, "How did you know?" He replied, "I could smell you reading. Let's go; we're burning daylight."

The little experience I had with trekking was with my best friend Gabby, out behind the Bay Village Apartments. We would roam the big empty field and blaze trails through the overgrown weed bogs hunting frogs. The water was smelly, the ground was broken up by earthmovers, and the sound of the South Bay never faded in our ears. Still, with a little imagination, we were Lewis and Clark in the wilderness, taking possession of the Louisiana Purchase. I was in the real deal now. The true wilderness pushed all-in on me. Was I going to call or fold?

The place my Dad had taken us was deep in the Sierras, about 50 south of Yosemite and 50 miles east of Fresno. The campground was called Sweetwater. That's about all I knew about it except that it took a lifetime to get there in the back of our station wagon. This place was God Honest Ansel Adams Wilderness Forrest. The pine trees were impossibly tall and waved about lazily in the afternoon breeze. The camp was situated in a lovely canyon with a stream bubbling overexposed boulders and forming clear shaded pools where trout would just sit there looking at you. The air was painfully clean—the sky, the purest blue with perfect little white clouds smiling down. The absence of city noise was deafening. My ears kept straining to reach the ambient traffic noise I had grown up in, but the only thing there was the whisper of the wind and the music of the water. When my mom or Dad spoke, it seemed like they were interrupting a symphony at its most tender moment. My Dad, El Jack, would sometimes stand beyond the edge of our camp and just stare off in the distance and listen. He was drinking in his heritage. This was the crack he was addicted to.

This explains why he overlooked how unprepared I was to follow when he tossed my two older sisters Margie and Kate and I out on the trail. Our big black Lab, Sarge, came along to bring up the rear as El Jack hit the water and started upstream. Dad bounced along like Tigger, just full of joy, and we tried to keep up. Soon Kate, Margie and I got the rhythm of rock-hopping. It was actually fun to bound along, making split second decisions as the boulders flew below our feet. Then we hit the cliff.

We came to a place where a lovely waterfall spilled over an edge about 500 feet up. Probably only 40 feet up, but it seemed like an insurmountable wall to me. Well, that does it, right? Nice hike; time to turn back, right? Nooo. A death-defying challenge to mount a lofty perch was irresistible to El Jack. He was determined to get to the top of it and bring all of us with him.

This is where the terror caught up to me. I was used to grappling over the salty scragg of the King Harbor breakwater with Gabby back home. But there, you are never more than a boulder high off the ground. As soon as my Dad got more than two-man lengths above the boulders below, I knew he was in the death zone. What if he slipped and busted his head open, and we had to scrape his brains back into his skull and drag his convulsing body back to camp? I've read enough Reader's Digest true adventures never to trust a perfect, peaceful moment. How can you know it isn't just a set up for the eventual disaster? I was already thinking about the back story that precedes the catastrophe. "He was a smart, good looking young man with a bright future ahead of him. How could he know that in the next instant, he would be fighting off bears in the mountains to save his badly injured father and terrified sisters?"

"Dad?" I said, "We had a great time. Maybe we should stop here and go back to check on Mom and Syndie?" He just huffed and attacked the cliff, clawing the slippery rock face as he explored a way up. Somehow, he got to the top. When he stood out on the edge, crowing like a rooster, completely exposed to the boulder death below, it made my stomach turn. But when he came down and rounded us up to make the climb, I panicked.

"You go on; I'll just stay here and take care of Sarge." I looked around but didn't see my black Lab. "Sarge! Where are you?" I called. He looked down at me from the top of the cliff. He had found some way up there through the brushy side of the canyon. Traitor. Even Margie and Kate were gung-ho. "C'mon, Chris, it'll be fun," said Kate. "Don't be a pussy. Look, Margie's already halfway up." I had no choice.

Kate scrambled up like a goat and joined her sister at the top. I went to the rock face and grabbed where Dad told me and put my feet where he showed me, and I began to rise off the ground. "Don't look down," he said. I looked down. I was already so high that if I fell, I would explode like a rotten tomato on the rocks below. Dad repeated, "DONT LOOK DOWN!" He put his hand under my butt and pushed me to the next hold. I grabbed hold while he scrambled around to a new position above me. "Just put your foot there and grab here, and you are almost to the top," he assured me. I looked down again. Without him below me, I was totally exposed. My leg began to shake. "LOOK AT ME!" he yelled. I began to cry. "PUSH UP!" He commanded. I pushed with all my might and rose another foot, far enough for him to grab my belt and pull me up to the top. I scrambled away from the ledge and tried to compose myself. I was embarrassed at my crying. Sarge came and licked my tears away.

When I stood up and looked out at what was on top of the waterfall, my trembling eased. A small lake stretched out before us, still as glass, reflecting the mountains in a perfect upside-down picture. A whisper of breeze rustled the leaves and made the grass of the meadow wave. El Jack stood there looking upstream, aching to go further, but he knew he had pushed me past a pivotal threshold and didn't want to test his luck. We just waded through the shallows to the meadow bank and skipped rocks across the water for a while.

"I'm sorry about crying," I said to Dad softly. He put a hand on my shoulder. "That's alright. Just the baby in you being pushed out by the man inside. You'll be alright. I won't mention it, and neither will your sisters." He gave my sisters a high eyebrow look like the Rifleman would, walking through the dust of Northfork, loading his Winchester. They nodded in agreement.

After an anxious climb down the falls, we rock-hopped back to camp. I strode up to Mom and Syndie like an Indian brave bringing in a buck. Mom was roasting chicken over the fire. She was relieved to see me alive and thankful for the man lesson Dad had given me. Margie and Kate told her where we had gone and what we had seen but nothing about my breakdown. Mom was so proud of me. I felt like a man. I think I even grew a few curly hairs down below.

When we got back to the South Bay, I still read and collected comic books, but I had a new interest in the mountains that we could just see through the smog, far to the east. I was infected. Reading tall tales is fun but living the adventure is way better.

Bullied at Center Jr. High

My first summer in Manhattan Beach was drawing to a close. Those damned back-to-school ads were all over TV. To make matters worse, I was about to begin Junior High. The days of one classroom, one teacher education were gone, baby, gone. As a new MB resident, I knew nobody. Gabby was off in Palos Verdes. I was on my own. I had no friends, no confidence, no fashion sense, and no idea how I would fit in. However, I was blessed with one gift; a fat, flabby, pink body that made me a prime target for bullies. I walked into my homeroom at Center Jr. High feeling like an antelope on the Savanna.

Jr. High is somewhere near the seventh circle of hell for most kids, so imagine how bitchen it was to be thrown to the dogs as a stranger. The culture at Center was very different than what I knew at Grace Wright in Torrance. GW was populated by the spawn of working-class apartment dwellers. I knew how to run with those rats. Center was hardcore surfer kids from MB. I could barely swim, let alone surf. All the kids at Center had grown up together, attended the same elementary schools, pre-schools, and day camps. They all played on Little League teams and surfed their brains out together every spare minute. That's what it seemed like to me. My gears didn't mesh with their gears, so I was invisible at school until my helplessness attracted the attention of a shark.

I don't remember his name, so I'll call him George. Typical bully. Short, pimply, with a complete set of henchmen that thought everything he did was cool. He sat three desks down from me in homeroom. He made fun of everything I wore to school. He ridiculed everything I did. In fact, I provided George a limitless banquet of bully fodder in which he gorged himself every day. I became quite stoic. My life at that time was miserable anyway, and George seemed to organize it. Instead of suffering from vague feelings of inadequacy, George gave me concrete reasons to believe I was ugly, stupid, and hopeless.

The only other class I shared with him was P. E. (lucky me!), and that's where George released his bullying art with passion. I had to undress before him to get into my gym clothes, and that's where my flabbiness found its real purpose. George and his henchmen were all lean, wiry kids who played ball or surfed all day, and I must have stood out like a giant white larva amongst their tanned, muscular frames. You can imagine what fun I had in that class all year. Reading this probably makes you feel like beating me up as well. I understand. Yet, all this was simply a prelude to a remarkable day that changed my life.

It was gym class, and George and his boys were in top form. We were dressed in our gym clothes and out on the asphalt basketball court choosing teams. The pool of un-chosen kids was getting smaller, and I was in the middle of it. No one would touch me for fear that the stink George had laid on me would rub off on them. The humiliation became excruciating. Finally, all the teams were chosen, and I was left there, alone. George came up from behind and said something I can't repeat and slapped the back of my head.

A bomb went off inside me. I spun around and roared a stream of incomprehensible utterances as I exploded into him. George was utterly shocked. I came after him not as a fist fighter but in an all-devouring, arm swinging, clutching mass of pure slobbering fury. I caught George frozen in horror, and he fell backward with me on top of him. I felt the breath get knocked out of him, and I began to organize my fury into pummeling his face with my pink virgin fists. About this time, the teacher pulled me off and sent me to the locker room.

I felt like I was walking upside down; I was so high on adrenaline. George must have regained some composure because he yelled after me that he was going to kick my butt after school in front of the flag pole. That news would have made my blood run like water before this day. Now it hit me as a chance to finish what I started. I was still hell-bent for fury. I was surprised how easily George folded up to my attack. I was surprised I had that attack in me. For the first time in my life, I was truly angry. Not upset, mad, pissy, complaining, grumpy, or put out; I was ANGRY.

After school, I went directly to the flag pole. I waited for twenty minutes. George never showed up. George never showed up again. He was still in school, in my classes, but he never showed up to me again, and I was definitely off his radar screen forever. I did, however, begin to show up on everybody else's radar. Bullies decided I was not worth picking on anymore. Word spread in school about my one-man riot. The stink was off me, and kids started accepting my presence in their groups just for the crazy factor. This incident had blown a hole in the granite wall that keeps nerds like me from ever fitting in. I was still a nerd, but I had claimed the ground under my feet and defended it. I just wasn't too sure what to do with it.

I learned right then that you don't have to actually win a fight with a bully; you just have to be willing to fight. If a bully pulls your pin, blow up in his face—every time. If you do, even if you lose the fight, you make yourself too expensive to fool with. Bullies are cowards. They will look for easier prey. Bullies had victimized me all through my years in Lake View Terrace. Back then, I paid off with what bullies want most, fear, whimpering, crying, hiding, and begging. No wonder they hunted me. I was the Gravy Train of Bully's Delight. There, in the schoolyard of Center Jr. High, I stood up to a bully for the first time, and the leak in my self-respect was finally repaired. I began to build equity, enough to try out for Mira Costa football later. I thank God for that fight with George. It was about the best thing that happened to me at that point.

A punch in the nose goes a long way.

Banished to North Redondo

I was ignorant of South Bay geographic snobbery until we moved from West Torrance to Manhattan. We heard things like, "Oh, you used to live in Torrance? Well, you are at the beach now." Or, "So you're finally out of the smog? How does it feel to finally breathe?" We picked up the message that we had 'arrived' pretty quick. We lived about a quarter-mile from the crashing surf, just over the hill. It was nothing but bleached out long hair surfer kids in our neighborhood. At 13 years old, I had just begun to realize it matters where you live. Everyone knows there is a right side of the tracks and the wrong side of the tracks.

By the time I started 8th grade at Center Junior High, life was shifting under me again. My dad, El Jack, got in a fight with our Manhattan Beach landlord, and we got evicted. Dad found a cheap rental just east of Aviation about halfway between Manhattan Beach Blvd. on the north and Artesia on the south. It was a two-story house just off the corner of Blossom and Graham. After only a year and a half in the Promised Land, we were headed to the Broken Promise Land (as in, "you promised we were going to live at the beach!) This was the wrong side of PCH, dangerously close to the Great Wall of the 405. But what choice did we have? El Jack was Captain Ahab, driving our ship on to pursue the Great White Whale of his ego.

North Redondo was Aviation High School territory, but El Jack wasn't going to let us become Falcons. No, we had to follow his footsteps and go to Mira Costa. This tactical decision ensured that I would have no friends that lived anywhere near me for all of my high school days. Not that I had friends, but it's the principle of the thing. Oh, well. We became commuters in every aspect of life.

Little did I know that while El Jack was navigating us into this backwater neighborhood in N. Redondo, he planned to jump ship. My Mom and Dad fought like jackals nearly every day. El Jack began to spend weekends at his Grandmother's house on Ruhland, where he kept a cab-over camper set up on the driveway. They said it was just a constructive separation, but I'm no idiot. Their marriage was a violent furnace where dreams came to burn. My mom was a prescription pill addict and an alcoholic, and El Jack was a self-righteous cocky jerk for the most part, so were we doodly doomed to be a broken family right quick. When I was a little boy, I used to think I could alter the inevitable outcome by being cute, weepy, and needy. It never worked. Now, as a young teenager, I could plainly see the disaster ahead like a train headed for a blown-up bridge. It was going to be ugly. Still, life never stops coming at you. Every day the sun rises no matter what, and you have to get up and solve the puzzle of life through your pain. If you were raised in a broken home, you know what I mean.

My cousins, the Jerand family, lived a few blocks to the north. They were no strangers to drama, but the prospect of our tragic Gypsy cart setting up nearby must have been delightful. My mom was already hitting them up for survival cash on a regular basis. Imagine how excited they were. "Oh, yaaay, the Lawlers have moved even closer to us." Kind of like a port-a-potty business opening upwind from you. Sorry, Uncle Bud and

Auntie Pat, we may be embarrassing relatives, but at least you get to pay for it for years to come. (Sigh...)

The way this house was arranged, all the bedrooms were upstairs. Margie and Kate had the back one, Grandma and Syndie had the middle, and Mom and El Jack had the master bedroom upfront. That left me to move into what would have been the den on the first floor. So that became my bedroom, but it still had to serve as the den at the same time. Our TV went in there, the sofa and a lounge chair. I had a single bed in the corner.

All in all, I was ok with it. By that time, I was a TV addict, so it was on almost all day. What there was was no room for were my drums.

They had to go into the garage. I was sort of getting over them anyway, so I didn't pine too much. Being a few years older, I realized what low-level drums they were: no Ludwigs, no Gretsch, or Tama, not even the good Japanese drums, Yamaha. Mine were just no-name Woolworth specials. I set them up at the back of the garage, but El Jack crashed into them, trying to back his truck in. He cracked the bass drum and bent my cheap ride cymbal. That was it. With no band to play with or even a dude to trade solos with, they never saw the light of day again. I had moved on to guitar anyway.

The Menagerie

One day my big sister brought home a white spotted puppy she named Oglethorpe. She was a mix of beagle, retriever, wiener dog, and basset hound. Kind of a mess. Margie named her after a Confederate General. O-Kay.. anyway, I thought I would never love a dog again after losing Scarapooch (another dog Margie named after obscure medieval characters). Scarapooch had died of distemper a year ago, ripping my heart out. But, sure enough, this dog bore a hole right through the scar tissue and drilled right into my soul. She anchored me as only a dog can, and I leaned hard on her as only a lonely boy will. We made no effort to keep her inside the house (or on our property, for that matter), so she roamed the street at will. She was so good-natured she became famous in the neighborhood. She never barked, was friendly to cats, and didn't give a hoot about squirrels. People knew Ogalthorpe when they had never even seen me before. She was my constant escort on countless hikes up to the little market on the hill at Robinson or out to Artesia to buy comic books. I never had her on a leash, and she never left my side. I didn't train her to do this; it was just her nature.

Well, apparently, we were not done adding to the menagerie. Margie brought home a white goose that she found injured at the Alondra Park Lake next to El Camino College. It couldn't fly and was bitter about it. It would charge and 'goose' you every chance it got. She named it 'Donald' (after some other obscure angry character from the Magic Kingdom), and it lived in the backyard. Donald would 'play' with Ogalthorpe by letting the dog chew on its wing. At least, that's what I told my little sister Syndie. Judged by the pitch and timbre of the honking, I don't think it was all that much fun for Donald. I would yell at Oglethorpe to let Donald go, and she would drop the wing with a 'whatever' look. Eventually, Donald moved in with the Hispanic family next door, where he fell in with a gang of Mexican chickens. Donald was much bigger, so he became their leader, El Quacko. His Segundo was the rakish, debonair rooster, Ronaldo. They had an understanding. Every dawn when Ronaldo crowed of his conquests, Donald would honk his approval.

When Donald moved out, a feral black cat (Miss Miniver) moved in. She was already pregnant, and so was Oglethorpe. She had her kittens about the same time Ogalthorpe had puppies. Miss Miniver was a hoary old alleycat, but her kittens were born sweet and gentle. All of them were black with white socks on their feet, a splash of white on the head, and the tip of their tails. They didn't know they were cats any more than Ogalthorpe's spotted puppies knew they were dogs. They mingled freely and thought they were all one big family. Watching them all play together in the back yard was the most amazing thing. That was cute for a while until the racket and chaos got crazy. When they got big enough to be adopted, I set up a stand in front of Alpha Beta with a box of puppies on one side and kittens on the other. I made a big sign that said, "FREE UGLY PUPPIES AND KITTENS TO FEED YOUR SNAKE". People came over to scold me for my cruelty in droves. When they saw the cute livestock looking up at them, they had to rescue one. They were all gone in two weeks.

With all this wildlife everywhere and El Jack gone, my backyard became a jungle of tall weeds, bare dirt, and junk everywhere. Gabby and I would hang out back there, shooting my airplane models with BB guns. We ran a fishing line from the roof to the far side of the yard, where we tied it to a stick, 2/3 up. A model plane with a plastic straw taped to it was run up the line and rested on the top of a tall ladder. When the 'pilot' took off by pulling back the stick and stretching the line, the plane would 'fly' down the wire. The 'pilot' could make the plane fly up, down, left, and right by pulling on the control stick. The plane would try to attack green army men and their fort while the 'gunner' would try to shoot it down with the BB gun. We took turns being the pilot or gunner until there was nothing left of my model planes but plastic scrap.

I know what you are thinking. You wonder if I ever shot any of the wildlife in my backyard with my BB gun. The answer is NO. Although, I did consider shooting Donald after he goosed me in the nuts one day. He wisely moved on before I recovered. I would have shot that cat-hole Miss Miniver if I could have found her. She had a BB with her name on it. But, after dropping her litter, she moved on to go slut it up in some other ally. Oglethorpe was off-limits. I was so in love with that dog. I would never think to torture or hurt her the way some young teenagers might. Long after Gabby had gone home and I was left alone for the next several days, Oglethorpe was still there, curled up beside me in my den-room while I watched reruns of That Girl and dreamed of Marlow Thomas curled up next to me. Marlow was beautiful, but she could never be as soft and sweet as that old dog smiling up at me.

Treehouse

In my backyard, we had a big Eucalyptus tree—the thing towered over the block. I got up one day and decided to build a treehouse in it. I had just finished reading Robinson Caruso, so I was fascinated with improvised construction. El Jack was mostly gone by this point, so there was no one to see (and stop) the catastrophe I was about to construct. Don't worry, I lived to write about it, didn't I? So it wasn't all bad.

I collected some 2x4's and fence planking and a bunch of nails and went to work. (God, I love 2x4's! Is there anything in the world that packs more potential for possibilities than a clean, straight, 2x4?) I nailed some pieces on the trunk just like I've seen in cartoons. 2-3 nails each. That should be enough to support the weight of a 165-pound kid, right? I had to put in many of these ladder rungs to get to the first split in the trunk, which was about 22-25 feet up. Then I had to climb up the trunk carrying the lumber and hammer and nails and wedge them in the branches to work on them. The blasted ladder rungs kept pulling out from the trunk as I climbed, but I just hammered them back in, no sweat.

Eucalyptus trees don't have many sideways growing branches to build a platform on, so I had to nail some 2x4's on the side to make a foundation for my' house'. Of course, I used slightly bigger nails for this, at least 4 for each board. One board was wedged in the split of the trunk. I didn't nail that one because I couldn't figure out how to. Then I started nailing the fence planks to the 'foundation' to form my floor.

It was a little hairy being way up there trying to hold on to everything and swing a hammer and all. I decided I needed a safety rope. So I tied a thin nylon rope to the branch, made a loop in the other side, and put it over my head. I put one arm through it; otherwise, it would have been a hangman's noose (duh). I figured if I fell, the thin nylon rope would grab me about halfway down to the ground and (cut me in half? Noo...), it would save my life. Safety first!

Well, I got my platform built, but it was pretty narrow, only about a foot and a half wide. It was getting dark, so I was running out of time to build a house on it. I was so excited about what I had accomplished, I wanted to spend the night in my Sky Palace, so I went to ask my mom if I could. She looked out the kitchen window at what I had made and thought about it... and thought about it. She wasn't a general contractor; what did she know about construction? She said, "Looks pretty high. Are you sure?" I just stood there wagging my tail (if I had one) and said, "I'll be alright, I promise. Please, please, please, PLEASE?"

"Go ahead, but if you kill yourself, I'm going to be pissed." She went off to have another smoke. I grabbed my Boy Scout cotton sleeping bag and a pillow, a bottle of Pepsi, a flashlight, and a Plastic Man comic book and began to climb.

One of my ladder rungs came off about halfway up, but I didn't care; I figured I would just jump to the ground from there in the morning. I got up on the platform and set up my bed. It creaked and teetered a bit, but I found the balancing spot and settled in.

176

Once I was in and quiet, I noticed that the tree was swaying ever so gently in the breeze, rocking me like a loving mother. From up there, all you could see were the tops of other trees in every direction. It was like being in the canopy of the rain forest of the Amazon, just beautiful. I felt so proud of myself made adventure. I read my comic book and slowly drifted off to sleep, dreaming of Tarzan.

I woke up in pitch black, having to go pee. It took a minute to remember I was up in a tree. I had to go pretty bad, so I quickly considered my options. I remembered the rung that came off, and I didn't want to try climbing down in the dark. I decided to 'make it rain'. I unzipped my bag and tried to roll over to get an angle, but the whole platform rocked over badly. I barely got it to stop and recovered the balance point, but in the excitement, my bladder betrayed me. I peed all over my sleeping bag. I couldn't stop. I just kept peeing and peeing and peeing some more until the damn thing was soaked. Crap! Now, what am I going to do? It's the middle of the night, and I'm 25 feet up lying in a giant soaked diaper. What would Tarzan do? Hmm... He would swing on a vine! The rope! I still had the rope tied to the tree. I decided to climb down, holding the rope, and when I got to the missing rung, just shimmy down the rope. I started down in the dark, descending like a blind monkey. When I got to the missing rung, I discovered I was still a good 15 feet off the ground, too far to jump. It's Tarzan time! I grabbed the rope with both hands and stepped off the tree into space. The skinny rope whizzed right through my hands, giving me rope burns, but it did slow my descent slightly, so when I hit the ground on my back, I only had the wind knocked out of me for 5 minutes. The rope had nudged the platform, so the pee soaked sleeping bag came down after me. It snagged a ladder rung (thank God), but it shook off a sprinkling piss mist that settled on me softly. I guess I made it rain after all.

I never tried to sleep overnight up there again, but I shored it up with a bazillion more nails and used it as my personal treetop retreat. From up there, I could see into the backyard next door. I would check on Donald (I mean, El Quacko) and make the Mexican chickens riot when I threw corn cobs at them. I finally tore it down when my little sister Syndie got big enough to climb up. I didn't care about my life, but I couldn't have her blood on my hands.

I had a chance to visit my old home a few years ago. The big tree was gone. Probably died from nail poisoning. But the memory is still there, about 25 feet off the ground.

Yo-Ho, Yo-Ho, A Pirate's Life for Me

I think it was the summer just after Center Jr. High had kicked my can down the road to Mira Costa that my Dad, El Jack, left my mom and re-married. He chose a lady who happened to be pretty wealthy. She was the daughter of a banker, I think. I'm keeping her and her family's identity hidden to respect privacy. They lived near the Strand in Manhattan, and she had a trimaran yacht anchored in King Harbor.

My Dad got swept up in a very different lifestyle than the one he left us in. He tried to stay involved, but you know how these things go; his new wife had four kids of her own, three daughters, and one son, just like my family. They were another Bizarro version of us. They were everything that we weren't. They had everything that we didn't, including our Dad. I think my El Jack felt terrible about the situation he had put us in so, he would throw us a bone (actually, one of her bones) now and again. One of the things he did for me was to let me use the dinghy from the yacht.

It was a tiny, unsinkable thing with a little sail. My best friend, Gabby, and I took it out one Saturday to kick around King Harbor like real sailormen. The boat was so small, the only way we fit was to lie in it, feet to head. Neither one of us had ever sailed before, so the New Wife's concerns were justified. We untied it and shoved off before she could think it through.

Once out on the water, the experience began to transform us. Aye, we found that the wind found its way into the bosom of our sail and carried us along to destinies shrouded in mystery. We divined that if we pulled the thingy and pushed the other thingy t'port or st'brord, we could bend our vessel to our will. We plied the waters up and down the harbor, making of ourselves a general navigational menace. Blast the civilities of privileged yachtsmen! We paid no mind to the regulations of maritime law (as we were ignorant of them); we were free of conscience and pursed our fancy with lustful abandon.

Only once did we tease the open sea where the deep grey rollers would flirt with our manhood, enticing us to draw near, so it could devour us whole and shit out our rotting corpses deep inside Davey Jones locker.

"'Tis adventure that beckons us out beyond the wall," says me swarthy mate, Gabby. "Shall we test the salt in our blood and the weight of our cannonballs? Shall we dance with the deep?"

"Nay," says I. "Why serve ourselves up as a codfish to Poseidon, when thar be caravels fattened with booty for the plundering just bobbing about inside the King's Harbor."

"Aye, truly spoken," says Gabby. "Bring 'er about and set the sheets for riches and glory, me bucko."

And so we prowled about His Majesty's harbor leveling broadsides of insults that would peel the varnish off a teakwood deck. Many a craft was forced to alter course because of our fearsome presence (and because we could not get out of the way). We terrorized one ship so dreadfully that their first mate surrendered two cans of beer to us in tribute. Gabby's draught was quickly guzzled down before I had barely opened mine. I was just about to swill me brew when 't blasted harbor patrol drew near, forcing me to drop me prize overboard. Gabby has never let me hear the end of it since.

Well, we were run off the sea by His Majesty's Navy, and we lost access to our plucky vessel. So, back to plowing potatoes on dry land? Nay! We found equally worthy vessels to continue our dominion over the deep. With our ballast sunk low in the middle of fearsome inner tubes, we continued our reign of terror. We plied the waves of the Colorado River, the Green River, Lake Gregory, and many other fearsome waters that shall remain nameless. All the while, singing our anthem (sung to the tune of 'A Pirates Life For Me', from The Pirates of the Caribbean at Disneyland.)

'Yo-ho, Yo-ho, a pirates life for me
  We sail the sea, the rivers, and lakes upon our inner tubes...
We think we're the salts of the Seven Seas,
  But we're just a couple of boobs...
Yo-ho, yo-ho, the pirates' life for me!

The Girl at the Back of the Bus

In 1970, I was thirteen years old, suffering my last year at Center Junior High and bumping along in a school bus to Leuzinger High School in Lawndale. This was a field trip to a special anti-drug program for all the area schools. The assembly was forgettable, but this trip was burned into my memory by an experience so intense, it still gives this old man goosebumps.

To my beach-centric world view at that time, Lawndale seemed like Mongolia. Who goes to school out here? It was on the inland side of Hawthorn Blvd, east of the Great Wall of the 405. Every beach kid knows that's just fly-over country until you hit New York. When we pulled up to Leuzinger, the building's graceful Classical architecture just looked to me like an Insane Asylum from Gotham City. This had to be where the Joker, the Penguin, and the Riddler sent their kids to school. I half expected Do-Whop groups to be singing around blazing trash cans, with leather jackets and greasy duck-tails. Sheesh. Dorothy is not in Kansas anymore. (Sorry, Leuzinger alumni. I'm sure you loved your school no matter how scary it was.)

We went into a big basketball court and sat through a boring presentation about drugs. There were some Dodgers, Lakers, and Rams athletes there trying to make us all straight edge. I think we all wished we had some drugs by the time it was over. Finally, it ended, and I couldn't wait to get out of there.

We all piled back into our busses for the ride home. I was sitting in the second row by the window. I was mostly a loner, so I had no one to banter with. I was just another body in the bus that Center Jr. High tried to inspire with these random trips to whatever. Then a bolt of electricity struck me.

Busses were lined up coming out of the parking lot of the school. Our bus was next in line to make the hard right turn to the driveway out. The bus just ahead of us had already made the turn but was waiting to move forward. That put the back window of that Crown bus squarely in my face. The round back window perfectly framed a lovely girl. She was looking directly at me.

To say she was beautiful is like saying a fish is wet. She had longish black hair with bangs in the front like 'That Girl' Marlowe Thomas, and clear black eyes. She looked at me and locked on with eye contact that harpooned my soul. Adrenaline surged through me, but I couldn't look away. I've never looked in the eyes of a girl for this long before, never been able to stand it. Yet, here I was, gazing at an impossibly lovely girl who was looking back at me! Something about the security of two bus walls between us made it possible for me to do what was unthinkable before.

Only her face was visible, so the rest of the scorecard was off the table. There was no way to judge her body or fashion sense, and, of course, there was no way for her to judge me. We were just two faces in the crowd, caught up in a private moment. In a few seconds, the adrenaline booster was spent, and it dropped away, leaving me in a weightless bliss where time stood still.

What was her story? Was she lonely? Was she looking for a boy like me? Would she 'get' me? Would she think I was smart, laugh at my humor, and be proud of me? What would it be like to walk the Strand as the sun went down and hold her hand, talking about the future, maybe sharing a smile, a kiss? The second booster ignited. I tenderly held her gaze. Her eyes opened my heart like a can of peaches.

I held my breath. I knew a once-in-a-lifetime moment was happening. I cherished it. She did not take her eyes off me. It was as if she was trusting me with her vulnerability, giving it to me alone. I resisted the urge to look behind me to see if another was the target of her interest. Instead, I embraced her with my eyes and folded my wings of compassion around her.

How could a girl like this not have a boyfriend? She seemed so peaceful yet, longing. Was she a loner like me? No one was distracting her, making snarky comments, pointing out targets to mock like so many other girl gaggle-packs were doing. No, she stayed with me, and her smile began to bloom. Not big and brassy, just soft and sweet with her eyes peering over the joy of her lips, inviting me to make a home with her for just this moment. I returned her smile, and we settled in.

I looked toward the grey facade of Leuzinger High and pulled the corner of my mouth up like, 'what choice did we have?' She rolled her eyes around, dropped her mouth in mock boredom, and yawned silently. I made a finger gun and blew my brains out. She strangled herself and stuck an imaginary spoon down her throat. We both laughed. She brushed her bangs from her merry eyes. I stroked the side of my hair and pointed at her with an approving nod. She tussled her hair slightly, smiled coyly, and mouthed, "Thank you". I mimed, "Where do you live?" She responded, "Hawthorne". She pointed at me and put her palm up to return the question. I mouthed, "Manhattan Beach" and thumbed westward. She nodded with understanding and made a frowning face. She was so pretty, even with a frown.

The bus began to move. She hunched her shoulders, pointed at me, and then herself and wound two fingers together with a sad smile. I nodded slowly, sadly. Her bus began to pull away. I waved. She blew a kiss. Then she was gone forever...

Hitting Bottom

The fact that I graduated Jr. High is a miracle. Or, a disgrace. Depends on what you're looking at; me or the school system. I was thirteen in 1970, and my home was in full meltdown.

In '69, my dad, El Jack, got in a fight with our landlord, and we were evicted from Manhattan Beach and landed in North Redondo near Aviation HS. Then he decided to leave my mom because they could not stop fighting. Mom was descending into alcoholism and prescription drug addiction. Grandma was bipolar and married to the sofa. My oldest sister, Margie, had jumped the rails and was a full-blown drop-out hippy. Kate, my middle sister, was outsourcing her family needs by latching onto her friend's families like a lamprey. My little sister, Syndie, was looking to me for stability while auditioning to be a Mexican so she could join the family that lived next door. That about sums it up. Is that melodramatic enough?

I tried to pay attention to school. When 8th grade started at Center Jr. High, I went to classes and tried to keep up. I missed one homework assignment after another, then got bad grades on some tests. I came home with an early mid-term report card that screamed trouble, but my parents never even looked at it. They were way too distracted by their personal demons and tragedy soaked marriage to notice. When I started the second quarter, I was too far behind and couldn't catch up. Despair set in, and I just got to the point where I wondered if anyone would care if I just let go of the wheel. I stopped doing the work and ran school into the wall and watched to see who would notice. Hello? Anyone out there? Crickets.

It was one thing to admit I couldn't keep up with algebra or care about social studies. It was another to realize no one was covering me. It's like I retreated from the front line bombardment and found that Headquarters was abandoned. Fear seized me. The school year rolled on. The administration tried to reach out to my parents, but they were ignored. My career at Center Jr. High ended with solid 'Fs' in my final report card. That's the only time that ever happened to me. I was too ashamed to attend my graduation. Still, Center kicked the can down the road. I think they called it 'matriculation'? Whatever. They matriculated my ass out of their responsibility and on to Mira Costa High School.

This moment of failure left me stunned and numb. I can remember entering summer with amazement. Was that last year a dream? Or did that actually happen? I had no one to reframe this disaster to keep it from branding me. How was I going to drag this dead year to Mira Costa? Like going to a party with a dead rat in your pocket. The children of Manhattan and Hermosa Beach were sun-blessed and successful. I am clearly not of their race. Would I even understand the language they spoke?

I stood at a crossroad. If I owned my failure, let it mark me, and followed the tracks laid before me, I would descend to the graveyard of wrecked dreams. I would be forever running down the rails trying to catch the train of achievement leaving the station. Yet, if I could somehow jump the rails and brick in the corpse of the last year, I might be able to hack a new path through the jungle in High School.

Something happened in the summer of '1970 that washed the doom of my failure away like a sandcastle. God put a little book in my path called "The Hobbit". Reading it was the last assignment I had ignored at Center. I still had the paperback. One night after dinner, I picked it up and started reading.

Before it spawned a bunch of movies and cheesy cartoons, The Hobbit was an epic book, first of its kind. It opened the door to the larger, three-volume world of "The Lord of the Rings". I devoured it all. I was enchanted by the language J.R.R.Tolkien used. It was English, but I had never heard it used this way. Over the summer, I would grab every chance to hide in my bedroom with a cup of Sleepytime Tea with honey that I imagined was first brewed by the Elves of Rivendell. I would eat Pop-Tarts that stood in for elvish 'lembas'. While I adventured through the Mines of Moria and the dark forest of Mirkwood, my self-image and life paradigm was overhauled by God.

What appealed to me about Bilbo and Frodo was a life not spent just working and buying but questing for a higher purpose. Hobbits were, in many ways, the least of the races of Middle Earth. They would have failed to meet the standards of the other races that inhabited their world, but they were not interested in competing. They were content and humble yet, still found their purpose and made a critical contribution. Along the way, they tended the garden of their tribe, loved their companions, and gave hope to every outsider who laid eyes on Tolkien's words.

All through the summer, I was immersed in the struggle for Middle Earth. When I finished the last book in my bedroom, it was late afternoon, and the gold tinted sun poured in my window thought dancing leaves. I choked up when I closed the cover because I knew I would never be able to read it again for the first time. As I fell asleep, Eric Clapton's 'Layla' was playing on the radio. The second half piano ballad invaded my dreams of Middle Earth. That dream gave me hope that my Quest was just starting. To this day, when 'Layla' comes on the radio, all the rich emotion of that memory comes flooding back.

I doubt that anyone will ever experience Middle Earth first by reading the enchanted English of Tolkien. The movies were too strong, too exciting, and too easy. What took me two months to complete, a movie watcher can consume in a few hours and think they have the gist of it—what a loss. There is an enchantment on Tolkien's written words that reward a virgin reader with riches from the deepest heart of Moria. If only they can experience this epic FIRST as a book, then its power to change life is undiluted. God used this experience to show me that no matter what has happened to you, every day dawns with a call to Quest. Every day is the trailhead to a new adventure. Life is not meant to be secure and stagnant.
A ship may be safe when it's tied to the dock, but that's not what it was made for.

Bilbo once sang, "The road goes ever, ever on..." my road led to Mira Costa High School.

Summer Before Costa

The summer of 1970 arrived without fanfare. For my whole life up until then, the beginning of summer was the greatest moment on the calendar. It marked the end of school labor and the birth of endless days of adventure, ease, and fun. Off came the shoes. Pants were replaced with cutoff jeans. Button-down shirts were stuffed in the closet, and t-shirts ruled.

This was the way I had greeted every summer up until then. This summer was different. A thick fog of anxiety drifted in and made breathing an effort.

I walked out of the ruins of my last failed year at Center Jr. High with no confidence I could do High School. My Dad was gone from my house, living in a camper on my Grandma Fergie's driveway. His attention was directed to the future, a new girlfriend, a new reinventing of himself that didn't include me. After all, El Jack was just my step-father, so what equity did he have in a chubby teenage boy who he couldn't understand. My Mom was drifting deeper into her addictions, My Grandma (who lived with us) was bi-polar nuts. Even Gabby was mostly gone, dealing with his own troubles and running with a crowd from West Torrance.

The shelter I took that summer was under the paradigm of understanding I received from the Lord of The Rings books. I had just finished them as my Jr. High career burned around me.

J.R.R.Tolkien reframed my life as an epic journey. My path led through many bleak landscapes and included several crucibles that would transform me into a different kind of man. I had to cling to this hope because otherwise, I was doomed.

You begin to understand how I used Frodo's epic quest as a Rosetta Stone to put the melodramatic aspect of my life in perspective. This was critical. I was not a failure, a loser with no hope but a traveler through tragic lands. One day I would arrive at the heart of my quest, play my role, and enter the destiny reserved for me by God. Without this understanding of my life path, I might have checked out.

I had grown over the last year to six feet tall. I was big but not muscular. Unlike the wiry surfer dudes who surf-paddled their arms into gorilla limbs, I had no athletic experience to speak of. Still, I looked like I would fill out a football uniform, so my family put great hope and heavy expectations on me to try out for football at Mira Costa. Those tryouts would happen in early August. That was the midpoint in a kid's carefree summer, so I had that hanging over me all through July.

My adolescent hormones were going crazy this summer as well. I could not swing a cat overhead without hitting a provocative image of a beautiful girl. From the bikini girls on the beach to the Farrah Fawcett posters everywhere, I had no rest. Even the Hot Dog on A Stick girl looked hot as the sun. My only hope was to burn off the energy with work, bike riding, long hikes, and the Three Stooges. This plan worked ok during the day, but at night, well... you know. Amazing I didn't light myself on fire.

This is where I'm going to stop this part of the narrative. In A Son of the South Bay II, I will pick up where I left off. I'll tell you all about my experience with Mira Costa, Gabby, and adventures that led me to strange lands and situations that would make Frodo's head spin. I hope you have enjoyed it so far. Please join me for a ride through High School into my early adult years in the next edition.

Special Bonus Section

Introduction

I've been writing stories about growing up in the South Bay for a few years now. All of you have shown me great love and appreciation, and I am very grateful. While these tales are pulled right out of my beat up memory, I stake no claim about the accuracy or authenticity of the facts included. Imagination has worked its way into most of them like termites. My sisters and friends (who were there when these things happened) all have their own version of reality. All my memories have been compacted over time and sometimes bleed into each other. Who cares? I just hope the tales I stitch together are fun to read. I offer this disclaimer in case I ever get interviewed by Oprah someday.

I didn't think I was writing a memoir when I started out. In fact, I had pretty much forgotten my Beach Cities years until I stumbled on these South Bay FB groups. Once I opened my mind, junk started falling out. I would dig up some memory, like a piece of broken pottery, out of an archeological site and ponder it. If it was inspiring, I would try to find connecting material. Then I would do my best to string a narrative together into something fun to read. I had to fabricate bits that were missing as they do with missing dinosaur bones to complete a full skeleton. So what you get is about 80% fact and 20% fiction. Hey, I'm not writing the Bible here, I'm just trying to give you a few minutes of joy and maybe stir your memories as well.

So, I've just about exhausted every significant memory I can dig up. All I've got now are leftover bits and pieces. I've decided to mop these up and string them all together into a sort of 'Dark Ride'; a story that will take you on a tour of fun little moments that happened in different times and places but that don't rise to the level of tales in their own right. I would consider this work a piece of fiction, with chewy chunks of actual facts mixed in (along with some Easter eggs that only So. Bay people will get). The recipe here is about 85% fiction and 15% facts. The characters are based on real people, but I'm changing the names to protect privacy, and so I can lie about what they did. The only exception is Gabby, my long time best friend from my youth who co-stars with me in this story. I don't think he cares if I lie about him (I know I don't) as long as the lies make him look better than he actually is. Lipstick on a pig? Yep, I can do that. Also, my immediate family shows up some.

It's going to be pretty long, so I'm breaking it into parts and releasing it in episodes like an old time radio serial. I hope you dig it. Don't hate me if you don't. I'm writing about three episodes ahead of what I post, so I don't even know where it's going to go. Mysterious, right? If you find your memory getting kicked like a beehive and you want to add some detail or nuance in the comments, I might use it in the episodes to come, so, in a way, we can all write this together. Don't worry, I might not give you credit, but I will always remember you as one of the heads I stepped on to climb up to my goal, a published Memoir.

Up for it? Then get in the little car, pull the lap bar down and let's take...

Episode 1 - To the Beach

I was 12-13 years old while I lived in Manhattan Beach ('67-'69). I didn't make any friends. This was partly because I was incompetent and partly out of some twisted sense of loyalty to my best friend from Bay Village in Torrance, Gabby. Hard to explain this reasoning, especially because 'loyalty' didn't stop Gabby from making all kinds of friends in my absence. He had a gift of relating to everyone. He still does. That's why he has roamed all around the world, joining tribes and making connections freely while I've milked my 3-5 friends and lived in the same house for the last forty years. I guess it takes all kinds. Gabby has been the gateway to the world for me in several ways. But back then, he was a dork, like me.

One Saturday morning at about 8 am, I rang him up to see if he wanted to goof around. He said sure; if I could get to him. He was cooking up some ideas that might work out. We planned to meet at 'The Box' at noon. This meant I had to make the trek from 4th Street Manhattan Beach (off Valley Drive) all the way to Torrance. I was between bikes at that moment; (my Stingray had been stolen, and my mom hadn't bought me my Schwinn Varsity yet), so I had a good hike in front of me. I threw on a t-shirt and cutoffs and old PF Flyers and set out. When I hit the sidewalk, I found a coke can and stomped it down to make a 'puck' to kick ahead of me. With this distraction, I can cover miles and miles.

I hoofed it down Valley to Herdondo and then up the hill where it turned into 190th. When I crested the Divide at Prospect, the whole inland South Bay spread out before me. The air had that familiar crust of brown smog that was absent near the coast. Man, I savored that familiar sight. Weird, but I associated it with some of the best times in my life up to that point. This brown air is the medium Gabby, and I worked in. To this day, I don't mind some smog. My wife, Susan, can squawk all she wants, but I don't trust air you can't see. How do you even know it's there? I'll take air that eats with a fork. That's what we got back in '69.

I walked south on Prospect to where Redondo Union HS sticks its butt out, then turned east on Del Amo to the elbow of West HS. I wondered if I would end up in switchblade rumbles with thugs from these two rival schools when I went to Mira Costa in a few years. We would all meet in the parking lot at TRW in the moonlight and fight to settle the bragging rights for the South Bay. Then we would celebrate with brewskis while we sang do-wop around burning trash cans. Seen it in movies and TV. Has to be true, right? I lost my puck in a storm drain while I walked south on Henrietta to Torrance Blvd.

I was dragging by the time I climbed that last incline on Henrietta that leads to Torrance Blvd. Finally, I turned east and walked past the Daily Breeze building and saw Gabby sitting at the tables outside the Jack in the Box (The Box). I was pretty dog tired by then, so I ordered a Jack Steak sandwich with extra secret sauce, fries, and a Coke. We sat down to make plans for the day. Gabby had been working his network of other friends and arranged a hangout at the little beach inside the Horseshoe pier at Redondo. So after that death march to get to Torrance, we were on our way back to the beach. I didn't mind. There were going to be girls there.

On the way down Torrance Blvd, we passed the Safeway (?) on the corner of Henrietta and spied a few stray shopping carts. That made the street incline irresistible. Long before 'Jackass' made it a thing, Gabby and I were shopping cart bobsled racers. We grabbed a cart and took it out to the middle of Henrietta, and jumped on board after the bobsled push. Gabby tucked inside the basket, and I hung over the back with feet on the back wheels to steer. We were in trouble as soon as I realized the rear wheels were free rotating, not locked in place. That made steering impossible. We careened down the street, spinning around until I (being heaviest) was butt first. It was still exhilarating abandoning ourselves to fate. Eventually, we found the curb down the street and ended up ass over elbows in a pile on the sidewalk. We laughed it off and left the wreck and headed to King Harbor.

At the crest of the Great Divide (Prospect), the Pacific Ocean opened before us. Of course, it's the same ocean that kisses the sand at 4th Street Manhattan, but it felt different. Maybe it was because Redondo lacked the hardcore surfer culture; the shore drops off too sharply to make surf-able waves. Maybe it was because Redondo is the terminus of Torrance Blvd that pumped the inland hordes west for their day at the beach. Whatever it was, Redondo had a decidedly chewy-spicy texture. I related to it as a Bay Village expatriate. I was still more at home with the smell of pier tar than surf wax.

We descended past PCH, past Veterans Park, and walked out on the pier. Seagulls squealed and wheeled over the Mexican and Asian fishermen on the short spur. Bonita were running, so they were happily jabbering over the Ranchera music coming from their radios. We veered right past the Hot Dog on a Stick and walked past Tony's with its swanky old folks leering at their spent youth walking by. When we got to the middle of the horseshoe pier beside Castagnola's, we leaned over the inside rail and looked down. The water was clear as glass and even had a reasonable swell to it. Gabby scanned the beach and spotted his friends camped on the sand. He yelled, and they waved back. There were two guys and two girls. They waved for us to come over. Gabby looked at me for a second, and I understood. We threw ourselves over the rail into the brine below. I wasn't crazy about this idea, but when you're on Gabby's Fun Train, you go where the Engine goes. Gabby knows how to make an entrance.

We had to swim a little way before we could touch the bottom, but then it was easy to roll with the waves and get to the shore. I dragged myself out of the water with my clothes clinging to my body-shame. I might not win a wet t-shirt contest, but I had a fair man-rack going on. This was not my most impressive moment. We were all just on the edge of puberty, so the guys were still mostly boys. The girls had not completely ripened yet; nevertheless, they were bonafide, card-carrying females, and this doubled the atmospheric pressure for me. I pulled my t-shirt away from my body but did not take it off as Gabby did. I wrung it out best I could.

On the sand were Carl and Roxanne, Dave and his sister, Jenny. They all clapped approval for our stunt. When the lifeguard came over and gave us a warning, it doubled the glory. Gabby soaked it in. He did most of the talking, working his posse like a boss. These were his friends, so I kept quiet for the most part. I tried to concentrate on the banter so I could come up with a snappy punchline to add, but it was hard because I couldn't get my mind (or eyes) off Jenny.

Jenny was a promise from the future. Like the rest of us, she was young and had not come into her gifts yet, but the promise was there, like gilded presents under a Christmas tree. Whoever's name was on the gift card was a lucky guy. She had long, straight, sandy blond hair and wore a twinkle in her eye that made you think she knew your secret. Her body spoke of a young boy up top, but her hips begged to differ. Pity the fools she left in her wake in about five years. She would make trouble for men a hundred yards in every direction.

I had to look away, or I was going to get terminally google-eyed. Someone suggested we play volleyball, thank God. There was an empty net nearby, and Carl had a ball, so we took it over. Three on three. I made sure to get on Jenny's team so I wouldn't have to stare at her across the net. (Also, I would get to stare at her backside when I was serving. I'm no fool.)

Carl was also on my team. Jenny and Carl were native beach kids, so volleyball was second nature to them. It was going to be a challenge to keep up, but I was determined to hold my own. Gabby served. The ball came long, and I almost stuck my arm out when Carl yelled, "OUT," and I let the ball hit out of bounds. Ok, I almost screwed up there. Carl served. I took my position next to Jenny and tried to coil in a ready stance. Carl popped it over, and Roxanne received the ball softly on her forearms, Gabby set, and Dave spiked to my side. I dove for it, missed it, but kicked a foot full of sand in Jenny's eyes. She cried out and fell to her knees. Everyone rushed to help. We tried to pour a cup of water into her eyes to wash them out, but it didn't work. Finally, we led her into the breakers, and she dunked and let the ocean rinse them. That worked better, but it ended our game. She came out blinking and tearing up, but she said she would be ok. Now, THAT'S the way Lawler makes a first impression.

Everyone was a little annoyed that I killed the game, but they shook it off. The day was too rich to waste. The guys went body surfing while Jenny and Roxanne laid out in the sun. From the waves, I could see them talking. I felt a little like because of me, the china was being moved to a higher shelf, so I stopped caring so much and returned to being a kid. I even took my shirt off and didn't care. The ocean resets everything.

When we pulled out of the water, I was hungry. "Let's get something to eat", I said.

Gabby replied, "You're hungry again? You ate a whole Jack Steak sandwich just a while ago."

"Are you my mother?" I said, trying to remember that I didn't care anymore. I put my shirt back on.

"Well, I'm hungry too," said Jenny, tossing me a lifeline. "A Jack Steak sounds good. What are they like?"

She looked directly at me. Adrenaline shot up my spine. This unlocked my mouth, and the first half-witty words leaning on the inside of the door fell in the room. "It's just a regular steak sandwich with Jack on it," I heard myself say. Horrified.

Everyone stopped and looked at me. The guys were shocked, Roxanne was aghast, and Jenny's eyes were trying to find the fire escape.

"Oh my god, Lawler!" said Gabby, cashing the check, "You are soo disgusting!" That broke the piñata, and the laughter fell everywhere.

"I didn't mean that! Shut up, you guys! I only meant it had Jack's Secret Sauce on it." The laughter went to howls. Even Jenny was rocking.

Carl, Dave, and Gabby added to the joke in ways I can't write about without burning your eyes, so I'll leave it there. I was so embarrassed I could have sprouted mushrooms. Yet everyone was rolling with gut busters. Eventually, there was nothing left but chuckles, and Roxanne swept them up with, "You're all so immature."

Can I recover from this? Jenny had every reason she needed to block me out, but she was laughing softly at my blunder. Not mocking me but laughing with a smile that radiated grace. In some strange way, I felt like I earned a little equity with her. Hmm.. how can I leverage it?

Episode 2 - Lure of the Dead

We all decided we were hungry, so we broke camp and climbed up the stairs over the breakwater rocks, and walked around to the back basin where the fish market was. A small fleet of fishing boats bobbed around in their moorings. The water was crystal clear in the basin and revealed an octopus garden on the bottom. Good sized opal eye perch swam around begging for scraps from the tourists leaning over the rails. The seagulls overhead cussed them out for the competition. The Doors' 'Riders in the Storm' spilled out of the kooky bar (the Sea View?) on the lower level, west side. Its big doors were open, revealing a shipwreck wonderland. A model train chugged along a track suspended from the ceiling that wound around all sorts of nautical oddities. Sawdust and peanut shells covered the floor. Dark figures in the shadows leaned on the bar. This must be where the sea gives up its drunk.

The fish market was a zoo of every form of life under the waves that man could eat. Everything was set out on ice or in tanks. People were ordering crabs, fried fish, shellfish, and even Sea Urchins. An Asian man received a plate with one of these dark, spiky bottom feeders that had its top cut off, insides cleaned out, but was STILL crawling across his plate! It shivered me timbers. We stuck to the fish sticks, fried shrimp, and fries.

While we were eating, Roxanne told us about her uncle, who worked at the Blue Bayou Restaurant attached to the brand new 'Pirates of the Caribbean' ride at Disneyland. This was in the New Orleans Square that Walt Disney built to capture the French Quarter spirit of Mardi Gras. Roxanne said that the menu of the Blue Bayou included crawfish and frog legs.

"No way!" said Dave, "Disney would never sell weird things like that. It's too family friendly."

"It IS authentic to the culture and history of the South," said Carl.

"So was slavery, but I doubt Disney has any slaves working in the restaurant," said Dave.

"I don't know," said Roxanne, wiping ketchup off her cheek, "my uncle says he isn't paid a lot."

Dave laughed, "Still, frog legs and crawdads? Even if that's true, I don't think they would sell a lot of it. Maybe it's on the menu just as a joke."

"What do frog legs taste like?" asked Jenny, "and what is a crawdad anyway?"

"A crawdad is the cockroach of the sea, and frog legs taste like chicken, with a kick," said Gabby, proud of himself. "Or, maybe chicken tastes like frog legs."

Roxanne had finished her fries and started in on mine. "Well, that's what my uncle said. It sounds horrible. I could never eat a frog leg thinking of all those frogs in tiny wheelchairs in the swamp."

"Yeah, that's just too dark for Disney," added Dave. "They aren't going to risk making a little kid cry just to be authentic."

I pulled my fries away from Roxanne. "I'm looking at that man over there eating a sea urchin while it's trying to run away, and it makes me want to cry. I bet the sea urchin isn't too happy about it either."

Everyone stopped and turned around to see. The Asian man was scraping something out of the inside of the urchin. He pulled a spoon full of goo out and then noticed us all looking at him. He paused, held the spoon up in salute, then ate it. A little dribbled down his chin. He dabbed it off with his napkin, then leaned back, and belly laughed at the horror on our faces. The urchin's spikes slowly waved with the memory of life. Gabby returned the man's salute by raising his coke, and we all tried to rinse that vision from our minds.

"All I'm saying," said Carl, "is Disney isn't all sunshine and rainbows. It has dark secrets. All big amusement parks that have secrets they don't want customers to know."

"Like what?" Jenny asked.

"Like the time someone fell from the gondola ride over Fantasyland and crushed a family taking pictures with Mickey Mouse." Carl punctuated his claim with the authenticating 'slow-nod'.

"That's just a rumor," said Roxanne. "My uncle said it never happened. That rumor grew from an accident where a woman dropped her purse on a kid below. No one got hurt, but the rumor mill started rolling."

"Then why are they closing the gondola ride down?" asked Carl.

Gabby answered. "Because too many clowns like Lawler and me were spitting on people below." Gabby and I slapped five. Roxanne rolled her eyes.

"Still, accidents do happen," said Carl. "Bad accidents. Like the kid who had his head cut off standing up in a roller coaster."

"Seriously?" said Jenny.

"Rumors! All rumors," objected Roxanne.

"It's NOT a rumor," said Carl. "My brother is a sophomore at Redondo. He works on the school paper. He showed me an old copy of the 'High Tide' from 1956. They wrote about it. Said the kid stood up to see the ocean, and his head hit a crossbar and got ripped off."

"That's a high school newspaper written by high school dorks," said Dave. "You can't believe anything they say. They just want blood and guts to sell papers."

"Where did that happen?" I asked." P.O.P. Is right on the ocean. I once rode that Sea Serpent roller coaster with my Dad when I was a little kid. It was rickety then. I can only imagine what a death trap it is now."

"Pacific Ocean Park is my favorite," said Jenny. "Remember the Banana Train ride? I was so scared of the volcano, I climbed all over Dave to hide."

"You spilled my coke all over me," laughed Dave. "I had to go the rest of the day looking like I peed my pants."

"No, it wasn't Pacific Ocean Park," said Carl, letting the twins' giggles peter out. He took the tone of a campfire ghost story. "No, no, no, kiddies. P.O.P. Is a.. happy place.. for sweet families who can't afford Disneyland. It's a place to make delightful memories with Hobo Kelly that they will all cherish for a lifetime. The roller coaster I'm talking about is the rancid Horror of the Harbor. Its lair is among lost souls... the ragged whores... the Gypsy fortune tellers and tattoo artists, the decrepit Carneys and drunken sailors that all creep along the Midway of the Long Beach Nu Pike."

All our faces were screwed up in disgust. Everyone was silent in rapt attention. Gabby spoke for us all when he whispered the echo, "Nu Pike".

"Yes, Nu Pike," continued Carl, "This bloodthirsty demon coaster is called the 'Cyclone Racer'. My brother says the bloodstains are still there at the top of the drop. It soaked into the dry wood and can't be cleaned off. When they try to cover over it, the paint rots and falls away. They finally had to paint the rest of the coaster red to match the bloodstains from that guy and all the others the Cyclone has murdered."

A moment passed... A seagull cried... A buoy bell rang in the distance...

Then Jenny spoke, quietly at first, then with rising intensity.

"You.. are.. so.. full of CRAP!" We all broke up laughing.

Dave slapped Carl's back. "Pure crap. But I give you a ten for storytelling."

Carl was proud of himself and half laughing along with everyone but also trying to salvage some credibility.

"That's what my brother told me. One of his friends works there in the summer and knows all the secrets. He told Jake that the Nu Pike management wasn't even sorry about that poor kid. They claimed that the guy disrespected the Cyclone, and so the coaster demanded blood. He was so mangled that his own family didn't want to claim him. They got one of the Gypsy witch doctors to sew his head back on, embalm him, and mounted his corpse in a midway ride. It's still there among all the horror mannequins."

We were all still laughing. Jenny pointed three times at imaginary 'evidence' and punctuated it with, "Baloney, Baloney, and Baloney."

Carl took one last shot. "Believe what you want. Anyone can go and see for themselves. The body is right there in the 'Laugh in the Dark' ride. The bloodstains are right there at the top of the drop on the Cyclone. But if you go, don't stand up, or you might be the next addition to the Pike."

"Then, let's go," declared Gabby. "Let's go see for ourselves."

"Really?" said Roxanne. "How morbid do you want to be?"

"Only morbid enough to find out the truth," Gabby replied.

Roxanne hedged. "It's gross. I don't think we..."

"I'm in," said Jenny.

"Me too," I said.

"Hell, yes," said Dave.

"Let's do it. Let's go ride the coaster and see the body and find out if we live to tell the tale," said Gabby. "C'mon, Roxy, the body might be cute."

"Geeze, Jenny? You really want to do this?" pleaded Roxanne.

"Beats getting sand kicked in your eye." Jenny gave me a wink.

Roxanne thought for a moment, looked a Dave, then caved. "Alright, let's go see the dead guy."

Carl leaned back with approval. "Excellent. Most excellent."

Dave said, "We gonna need money, we've got to set a date, then figure out how we're going to get a ride to Long Beach and.. we're going to need permission from our parents. We all have some work to do. I say we do what we can this week and then meet back here next Saturday to plan. Sound good?"

Gabby put his hand in the middle. "To the corpse of Nu Pike."
We all put our hands in the middle. "Dead guy on three.. one,
two, three... DEAD GUY!"

We hung out for a little while longer, climbing around on the
rocks of the short spur of the basin breakwater. Gabby and I
were used to climbing inside the boulders through the caves and
tunnels. It would have been fun, but we couldn't keep our minds
off the Nu Pike. After Dave slipped on a rock and scraped his
knee pretty good, we decided to call it a day.

We walked back to the fish market and parted ways. My path led
north back to Manhattan Beach while the rest of the gang moved
off towards Redondo and Torrance, laughing and goofing off as
they went. Inconsiderate, right? The least they could have acted
like the party was over. Instead, the festivities marched on like a
Mari Gras krewe. Loneliness put an arm around my shoulder and
whispered, "That's not for you. Get moving."

I walked along the little boardwalk next to the marina, thinking
about how I would accomplish The Mission. Oh, yeah, and all
the Nu Pike business too. The Mission was clear. How do I get
Jenny to see me through the crowd? What will I do if she does
see me? What will I do if she sees me but decides to pass? My
stomach flipped a little. Damnit! This is exactly why I DON'T
play this game. I'm already up this cliff a ways with nothing but
rocks below. It's slippery going, and I don't even know what's at
the top. No wonder Mr. Spock leans into his Vulcan side. That
side is neat, organized, logical, and safe. The human side is a
dangerous tangle of sorrow and delight, all rattling around in a
Gypsy cart. Not safe. Not safe at all.

Episode 3 - Any Port in a Storm

Just past the King Harbor marina, I passed the Seaside Lagoon, a man-made swimming pool with a sandy beach built for families that like the ocean but not what comes with it. Peter and Gordon's 'World Without Love' was lecturing me from the PA system. The Lagoon shore was full of moms laying out on blankets and talking at each other in small groups while their children played in the water that was probably half kid pee. Is this what's at the top of the cliff I'm climbing? Some of those moms still looked pretty hot. Some of them, just south of 'hot' and falling. I guess that's what having kids do to a girl. They eat out the inside and leave the husk behind. And where are the dads? Probably off working to fill their wives with reasons to live while they ogle lost chances. You know what? I just need to shut up and stop thinking. I'm usually at my best with my brain turned off.

Past the Lagoon, I walked along the path between the marina where the big yachts were moored and the fancy restaurants that faced the power plant. Once I got past the commercial zone, I picked up the south end of the Strand in Hermosa.

Is there any better place for a teenage boy to walk on this planet than the few miles of Strand of the South Bay beaches? The late afternoon sun spilled gold over everything facing west. Old Man Sol had shed his fire but was still warm as a grandfather's hug. Hardly any reason to wear clothes. Thankfully, the girls agreed.

Their bronzed brothers with bleached mops hung loose along the low concrete wall that held the sand away from the houses. I wondered if I would ever join that tribe.

Music poured from open doors all along the way. Mid 60's surf music like "Wipe-out", "Mr. Moto" and "The Nobel Surfer" had pretty much faded. Complicated rock was taking over. The Rascals, "Groovin", the Association's "Never My Love", and "Up, Up and Away" by the 5th Dimension each tinted my thoughts and made me consider life's colors. Even simple rock bands like the Beatles, the Stones, and The Beach Boys were not just picking teenage pockets for their record money but invading hearts with new ideas. The warm summer air was scented with "Incense and Peppermint" that had me looking for "Windy", savoring "Michelle" and wondering if she would "Light My Fire". I thought about Jenny all the way and knew I was a "Believer" in that "Brown Eyed Girl" and asking, "Wouldn't It Be Nice." The feast for the eyes and the musical current kept me floating up the Strand.

I stopped to use the public beach restroom at 22nd Street, a ways past the Hermosa pier. I stepped very carefully straight up and down as I entered. The wet concrete floor is treacherous. With all the water, suntan oil, kid pee, and other slop, it's like walking on greasy ice. You always take your chances sliding on whatever that slimy mixture is on the concrete floors. A slip and fall onto the surface of that Petrie dish of horror from a thousand beachgoers would be terminal. I mean, you wouldn't want to live anymore after coming face to face with that. Better to be put out of your misery. Even if you threw yourself in the ocean and scrubbed your skin raw, you would never clean the gags out of your mind. I was thankful that at least I had shoes on. It's hideous to do this with bare feet. Feeling a bit better, I checked my money and still had a buck fifty, so I hit the Green Store for a carrot juice to flush that memory out of my head. Recharged, I made 4th Street, Manhattan in no time.

I turned inland and climbed the slope to Crest Dr., then dropped into the pleasant little valley hiding in the lee of the hill. My dog, Scarapooch, was barking and wagging for me, chained to the front yard. He whined a little as I pet him. That's when I heard something crash into the wall from inside. I cracked the front door and peeked in to see my Dad and Mom locked in a verbal Donnybrook. They didn't notice me at the door. Mom was half crying and half raging, and El Jack was giving back twice as good as he got. I saw Syndie, my little sister peeking out from our room behind the kitchen, crying with fear. I didn't want to walk right through the fight, so I went around to the little lanai on the side of our house and came in through the screen door. Syndie ran to me, and I picked her up and took her out on the patio, and closed the door behind to mute the sound.

"Where were you, Gaga?" she asked me through her tears. Syndie was six years old. She has called me 'Gaga' since she was a baby. I don't know where my older sisters were, but it broke my heart to think of my little blond curly head alone in the house with all that going on. As soon as I had her outside on my lap, she settled down and played hard with her Raggedy Ann doll. She kept talking but never took her eyes off her worn-out doll.

"Mommy threw Grandma Fergie's chicken at Daddy, and it broke on the wall. I wanted to watch Romper Room, but they were too loud, and I couldn't hear Miss Mary Ann. Daddy said he was going to move away. I tried to tell Daddy no, but he pushed me away and kept fighting with Mommy."

I should explain about the chicken. My Grandma Fergie gave my Mom some of her prized porcelain tchotchkes. Grandma had a bazillion of these on display in a hutch in her living room. Grandma Fergie is my Dad's grandmother, so Mom made a big deal about keeping them safe. These colorful, glossy sculptures are irresistible to Syndie, so Mom had them on a shelf up high to keep them out of reach. I guess there's one less porcelain Rooster to worry about now.

Fights between my parents were not uncommon. Margie, Kate, and I all developed different ways of dealing with the violence when we were toddlers before Syndie was born. Oldest sister Margie would get right in between Mom and Dad and try to broker peace when she was just a runt. It sometimes worked but usually didn't. She became scarred with that exposure to anger that plagued her into adult life. Swim-bun was an escape artist. She always maintained a network of friends she could run to for shelter. She wisely outsourced her family needs. My way of surviving was the Bubble.

I didn't have friends I could hide with, and I was too young to get in the mud like Margie, so I developed the Invincible Bubble of Solitude to retreat into while all hell was breaking loose. I would sit in front of the TV and drill into whatever program was on and get lost in that alternate reality until the storm blew out. I don't know if it was the best way, but it helped me survive. I tried to teach Syndie how to make a Bubble. She was trying to do that with Romper Room, but I guess the fight was too intense.

I felt bad for not being there for her. I held her on the lawn chair as the sky darkened, but the noise from the fight was getting crazy, and things were being said I didn't think she should hear. We got up and walked out to the front yard. The fight was so loud it could be heard five houses away. Syndie and I walked up the hill to Crest to get away from it. We stood there and drank in the ocean view. The sun had just disappeared below the horizon. The scudded clouds overhead glowed insane orange-red against a velvet blue sky. You would think that such rich beauty would put out every fire of human stupidity, but it never did. However, it did remind me that the stupid below cannot corrupt God's beauty and majesty. He has a bubble of His own.

We sat on a low wall of post pilings in front of someone's house and watched the fiery curtain of Glory slowly put the beach to bed while listening to the Beatles' "Sgt. Pepper's Lonely Hearts Club Band" playing inside. So Bright and optimistic. A perfect alternate reality. Syndie and I shared a Bubble for as long as the album lasted. Then we headed back home because the street lights came on, signaling the universal curfew for all kids that grew up in the 60's.

Mom met us halfway up our block. She was frantically looking for Syndie, who had disappeared from the house (because I took her) during the fight. Dad had stormed out without even knowing Syndie was gone. Finding us walking back home together, extinguished her panic and let her fall back into exhausted tears as she scooped her baby in her arms. That made Syndie spill her bucket. I shepherded my broken family back to our house and inside behind closed doors. Mom asked me if I could take care of dinner and get Syndie ready for bed so she could lay down for a while. I knew what that meant. I said yes, and Mom retreated to

her bedroom and closed the door. We wouldn't see her again tonight. I made macaroni and cheese with hotdog slices, and we ate it, watching The Newlywed Game, then Get Smart.
During Get Smart, my sisters came home and went to their room, and closed the door. Music from a brand new underground FM station, KMET, leaked out. Syndie and I didn't see them the rest of the night either. Syndie fell asleep on the couch, and I put her in the little bed on the other side of our bedroom. I stayed up until 'Mannix' was over, then I cashed out the day and tucked in.

I lay there with my eyes open. Did El Jack start out googley-eyed over Mom the way I was over Jenny? How long did it take before sand got in the gears? No way am I ever going to let that ugly anger get into my relationships. Sigh... That's the kind of oath a green pubescent will make while he's experienced nothing but knows everything. It's romantic, hopeful, and beautiful; the stuff all those love songs written by teenage rock bands are about. For the other side of the deal, you have to go to classic Country music. That's where the story of the broken porcelain chickens are told. Battle-scarred Love veterans sing it like it is. You lose the girl, lose the job, your dog dies, and only Jack Daniels understands. Still, everyone gets to take their best shot, and I still want in. As I drifted off to sleep, I put my Bubble on autopilot and looked for the next foothold on the cliff I was climbing.

Episode 4 - Show Me The Money

I woke up the next morning with Syndie curled up at my feet. She was dug in and sprawled across the foot of my bed the way a cat will when they are perfectly secure. I tried not to wake her up, but she stirred and sat bolt upright, rubbing the sleep out of her eyes. She was so cute in her onesie footer pj's. I guess she didn't want me to get away without her.

"Is Daddy going to move away?" she asked. She must have been thinking about this all night. I didn't know how to answer her because I had seen my Dad move away and move back several times while I was young. This was the first time Syndie was old enough to be aware of the drama. I deflected.

"I'm not going to move away," I declared. "Whatever happens, you are going to be stuck with me." This seemed to reassure her, although it's a dicey thing to make yourself the life raft in someone else's storm. But when I looked at my little curly blond-haired monkey, everything in me seemed to pledge itself to the cause. This was a curious moment for me. It marked the first time I became aware of the difference between the strong impulse to seek 'satisfaction', as Mick Jagger would put it, and the nuclear impulse to BE satisfaction. That is, to serve, protect, pull someone under the shelter of your heart, and work to make them secure. This is how you water a woman (even a little one), so they will grow and bloom.

This little revelation was stunning. I realized that when I looked at Jenny with the eye of a ravenous wolf, I was just human. Yet, this other, far stronger impulse was what would make me a Man.

I got up and poured a bowl of Cocoa Puffs for Syndie and me, and we sat down to watch cartoons together. All the while, I was thinking about what I needed for our expedition. I needed money, a ride to Long Beach, and my parent's permission. I couldn't wrap my head around how I would ask for permission from my parents while their conflict was burning. A ride was dependent on their consent, so I focused on what I could do; make money.

We didn't get an allowance back then, so I had to scratch up the cash by my own wits. I had about $1.75 in the pocket of my jeans. I figured I needed at least $20, preferably $30 to pay for admission, rides, food, and peacocking expenses for Jenny's sake. That's a tall order. If I had known back then what I know now, that keeping a girlfriend is more expensive than owning an English sports car, I might have turned gay on the spot. Or become a Shaolin Monk. Or maybe a pimp (if you're going to get involved with girls, you might as well get into management). Alas, I knew nothing back then. God doesn't let any man know what he's getting into with a girl or they would run away screaming into the night, and the human race would have died out long ago. So, I focused on the vision of Jenny's pretty face until my mind got sparkly, and I was willing to work.

My Dad, 'El Jack', (as he liked to be called by his posse) had already left for work by the time I got up. Or, maybe he never came home last night. He kept a cab-over camper set up on stilts in my Grandma Fergie's driveway to hide in when married life got to be too much. He might have spent the night there. That camper was about the most bitchen man cave I ever saw. It had a small TV, radio, kitchen, bed, and stash of Playboys under the mattress that El Jack didn't know I knew about. He never let me stay there. Good thing. I might have lit myself on fire. Anyway, Dad was gone, so I had to think of something else.

When Mom finally came out of her bedroom, Syndie released me and latched on to her mommy like a baby Kangaroo, so I was relieved of duty. Mom didn't say much. I think she had a hangover, so I didn't press her. I shifted gears.

I got dressed and chewed my financial problem. I worked down the list of every money tree I knew. First, I checked under our sink for bottles I could turn in. We had about five big Coke bottles with 10 cents each and a dozen smaller RC Cola bottles with 3 cents apiece. I gathered them up in a paper bag and hit the street. I stopped off at several houses along the way to the Safeway on Manhattan Beach Blvd to beg for bottles (for a 'school project') and collected three bags full. Safeway gave me just under $5 for the lot.

When I got home, I grabbed my sand sifter and dragged the beach near the Manhattan Pier where the tourists come. Tourists aren't used to how the beach can pick your pocket and hide your valuables in the sand. They don't have the lore and practices down that locals do, so the sand around the pier is usually rich sifting. Of course, I'm not the only one who knows this. There were other treasure hunters waving metal detectors and dragging sifters to compete with, but I still managed to dig up a wallet with $7 inside and a few coins here and there.

The next day, I walked down to the Hermosa pier to drag the sand and check my secret spot. There is a place on the Strand where nature's forces tend to drive change in-between the pier footings. I call it "Aladdin's wallet". I pulled $2.25 out of there, another $3 from sifting the sand, and $2.75 from just walking around the pier area looking down. People drop change all the time, especially near the Taco Bell, where they walk up still wet from the surf to buy burritos. That brought my total to about $15 bucks or so.

The next morning, I called my Grandma Fergie, who lives on Ruhland in North Redondo right across the street from Madison Elementary. I asked her if she needed her lawn mowed. She probably didn't, but she said yes because she never passes up a chance to enforce Idaho toughness on a soft California boy.

I hiked up 2nd street hill past Sepulveda and down into the 'Tree Section' of Manhattan. I turned south on Peck and walked to Ruhland, which is right there where the Mira Costa High School football field is. Little did I know how important that patch of grass would be in years to come. I turned East on Ruhland and hoofed all the way past Aviation Blvd. to Grandma's house. Hmm.. 'over the hill and through the woods, to Grandmother's house we go...' no need to wonder if the Big Bad Wolf was waiting for me. Grandma Fergie was the Baddest Beast in the woods. Yet, she loved me like a Grizzly loves a cub.

Grandma Fergie is the only one on the planet that can call El Jack "Buddy". She is actually my Dad's grandmother. Dad has always been 'Buddy' to her since he was a runt trailing barefoot with his little brother Johnny in the woods of Idaho. I think she was the original American Tiger-Mom / Grandma. She took over from my Dad's actual mom (my Grandma Opel), who got remarried to a guy that didn't want the step-dad job. Grandma Fergie cracked the whip on Dad and didn't mind doing the same to me.

When I finally got to her humble three-bedroom cottage across the street from the elementary school playground, I was tired. I went to the driveway where El Jack's camper cave was standing and knocked on the door. Dad wasn't there, but Grandma Fergie heard me and opened her kitchen door with, "Buddy's gone, but I'm here, so come inside, sit down and eat pancakes." She sat me down at her little kitchen table and fed me a stack of the best pancakes ever made. (Years later, I learned her secret. She adds crushed Cornflakes, sugar, and a pinch of salt to the batter and spins it all in the blender. Amazing transformation. (Try it, and you will never go back). Once I was sufficiently carbed up, she kicked me out to her back lawn. It was the size of a football field (to me) with a grove of orange trees running down both sides. You will never see a splash of land like that in the South Bay without a McMansion or two built on it now. She showed me where an old push-reel lawnmower was and said, get to it.

"Where's the Briggs and Stratton, Grandma?" I asked, all hopeful-like. She had an excellent self-propelled mower with an extra-large catch bag the last few times I came to mow.

"Crapped out on me. Your Uncle Johnny's fixing it at his place. He'll get it running in a day or two."

"Well.. maybe I should come back in a day or two when it's fixed?"

"Or, maybe you should stop whining, take off your bra, and get to work like a man. The catch bag is next to the mower." She punctuated her sympathy by letting the screen door slam closed.

I pulled the mower out to the concrete patio just off the lawn and looked it over. It was old like she brought it from Ben Cartwright off the Ponderosa, but it was well maintained. The blades had been sharpened. The cutting edge gleamed where it had been ground. It was oiled, and the works spun smoothly when pushed. The reel blades sliced against the cutting bar with a satisfying scissoring sound. I hooked the bag on and pushed it out onto the lawn, and it harvested the grass with little resistance. My whimpering ceased. It was actually a sensual pleasure to push the mower along, making the grass cascade out the back like a green waterfall. I was all the way down the lawn before I realized I was working.

Hmm... tricky Grandma Fergie. She had fooled me into tasting the sweetness of working with well made, old school tools the way farmer boys from Idaho did. It was addicting. I noticed that when I came back up the lawn, the grass left a fresh pattern running the opposite way. I emptied the bag and began another run. I tried to keep my runs perfectly straight and slightly overlapping the previous line. The opposing strokes left a beautiful, alternating pattern on the lawn that would make the groundskeeper at Dodger Stadium proud. The lawn art was adorned with tight circles around every tree. I had cut my last circle when Grandma came out with a pitcher of 'Arnold Palmer' (half sweet ice tea/half lemonade). "Time for a break," she said.

"Not before I edge the patio," I heard myself say. "Where is your edger?"

Grandma pointed to the shed with a Mona Lisa smile on her face. I grabbed that edger and cut a perfect trim along the concrete. She gave me a big glass of AP, and I drank it down without taking my eyes off the lawn. I was drunk on pride, and Grandma knew it. "What do you think?" I asked.

"It'll do."

"How about the front lawn?"

"Go ahead."

My heart jumped just a little. This thing that I HAD to do had transformed into something I GET to do. Mowing the back lawn was a feast of achievement. I mowed the front lawn for dessert. It was savory. When I was done, I hosed off the mower and oiled it, and lovingly tucked it into bed in the shed. Grandma Fergie had a big sandwich waiting for me in the kitchen. Ten bucks was sitting right next to it. After kissing my Grandma goodbye, she went back inside, and I hit the street, high stepping all the way back to Manhattan.

Grandma's sawbuck brought my total to about $25. All I needed was another good score, and I would be irresistible to Jenny. Nothing looks so good on a guy like a bulging wallet, right? I didn't want to show up with 'piggy bank' money; I wanted to make it rain like a sailor on shore leave. Time to get my mule on and work for my Dad.

Episode 5 - Boyz in da Hood

Flush with my success in the lawn mowing racket, I called Gabby that night to check up.

"How are you making out with money?" I asked

"Not so good. Been slim pickings here," he replied. "How much you got?"

"I'm almost up to $25."

"Twenty five bucks? Geeze, Lawler, how'd you do that? You sell a kidney?"

"Just old fashioned hustle. I cashed bottles, dragged the beach, and mowed lawns. What do you have?"

"Seven dollars left over from my birthday money," said Gabby. "I'm in trouble."

Just then, My Dad came in from work.

"Hang on," I told Gabby, "I've got an idea." I put the phone down and yelled down the hall. "HEY DAD! Got any work for a couple of donkeys? Gabby and I need cash."

The reply came from the bathroom. "Nope, I'm just about done... wait a minute. I've got a house with construction trash that needs cleaning. Do you want to do that? It's a lot of trash. I'll pay $20."

"Each?" I asked

"What? Are you guys Union?" he pleaded. "This isn't New York, you know. But, sure, you do a good job, I'll pay $20 each."

I spoke into the phone, "My Dad has a cleaning job to do at a house. You want to do it with me? Pays $20."

"Let's do it," said Gabby.

I yelled at Dad, "We'll do it. When is it?"

"You can do it tomorrow. It's an all-day job. I'll drop you off in the morning and pick you up later."

"We're in," I yelled back to Dad. "Can we pick Gabby up on the way? He's in Torrance."

"OK, I've got to pick up some stuff at work first, then we'll get him on the way. Tell him to pack a lunch and be ready at 8 am," said Dad.

"Got it," said Gabby, listening.

Awesome. Got to love it when a plan comes together. With work set up, I subtly turned the conversation to a more pleasant topic.

"Have you heard anything from the others? How are they doing? What about Jenny? Did she say anything about me?" I bit my knuckle.

"Slow down, Moondoggie, Gidget's not going anywhere," came Gabby's answer. I could tell he was enjoying my angst. "She and Dave already have their money. So does Roxanne. They just asked for it from their Dads, and the old geezers rolled over and gave it up without a fart. I don't know about Carl. I haven't talked to him yet."

"What about Jenny? Did she say anything? I mean, about me?"

"Geeze, Lawler, are you really going to be pussy-whipped right out of the gate? She didn't say anything; there's nothing to say yet. You barely met her. Seriously, you've got to mellow out. She is choice, but she will bolt if you puppy dog her. She knows you're interested. Let it be. Play it cool."

"She knows? How would she know?"

"You kidding me? We all knew. Your tail was wagging every time she looked at you. Trust me, she knows. She is considering. Don't spook her off."

"Maybe the work will be good for me. Get my mind off it. We'll see you in the morning."

"Later," said Gabby and hung up.

I rolled out of bed at 6 am, washed up, ate Cheerios while watched Gumby on TV. What a weird concept, right? A squared-off clay dude with no clothes that hangs with a donkey. Still, I can't look away. I made a lunch worthy of a feast. I crafted a Wonder Bread sandwich of baloney and cheese with lettuce, pickles, and thin tomato slices topped with salt and pepper that was magnificent. A bag of Fritos and 4 Oreo cookies (fat boy has to have his sweets) and it was ready. We were out the door by 7.

We drove El Jack's beat up 62 Econoline van down to Redondo Beach to his shop.

"How are things with you and Mom?" I asked

"It is what it is," was his response.

Not exactly encouraging. El Jack married my mom when I was one year old. During my lifetime, he had separated from our family 4-5 times. Life went to hell during those separations. Mom just couldn't cope, and her addictions got worse. She leaned on me to be the Man even when I was five years old. That used to be flattering. Now that I'm older, the weight of being the Man of the house would be crushing.

"Seems like you guys made up," I said, hopefully.

"Not really. We just moved on. You can't stop every time you get a dent in the fender."

"That was more than a dent the other night."

"What do you know about it?"

"I came home while you were fighting. I don't think you noticed me take Syndie out, and you were gone by the time I came home."

"Sorry you kids have to go through that. It was a real shit storm."

A few streets passed in silence. Then I asked the $64 question.

"Are you going to move out?" Adrenaline shot up from my gut and squirted a tear out before I could stop it.

He noticed. He sighed. "Not yet. I wasn't raised to quit. I've still got some tread on the tires." He kept his eyes on the road so I wouldn't be embarrassed by wiping my eyes. I was grateful for that.

We pulled into the driveway of Gardena Carpet and Floor Covering just south of Torrance Blvd on PCH. He picked up something from the office while I loaded some tools and a cooler in the back. He got into a conversation with his old buddy Bob Gumm (also a floor man), who was loading a carpet roll. (Many years later, these two would own a roadhouse bar near Lake Perris called "Dad Gumm's". If you were a biker cruising your hog out on Hwy. 74 in the late 70's, you might have hung out there). When they were done, we took off to pick up Gabby.

Gabby was outside when we pulled up. No one will ever accuse Gabby of being late for anything. Punctuality is a gift he tried hard to give me. I was slightly embarrassed that it was 8:15 when we picked him off the street. He had a lunch bag with him. I moved to sit on the engine cover so Gabby could have the passenger seat. The engine under the thin cover was not only loud; it was hot and hard-boiling my eggs until I put my Dad's Thomas Bros. map book under my butt.

We drove north on Hawthorn Blvd. I kept expecting my Dad to turn west at some point to get to a house in the South Bay, but instead, he kept driving north. I guess he couldn't afford to buy a flipper in the South Bay. Can you believe some of those houses cost more than $100k? I know, right?

When we passed the Great Wall of the 405 freeway, I started to get concerned. We continued north all the way to the Imperial Highway in Hawthorn. This was before the 105 freeway was built over the neighborhood where The Beach Boys were raised. It was a middle-class area, not too unlike Torrance. Hawthorn was a foreign land but allied to the South Bay thanks to all the Wilson boys' surf music. I got nervous when Dad turned east on Imperial and drove into the hinterlands beyond. I bit my lip when we got to Crenshaw and turned north, and kept driving. I looked at Gabby, and he was in shock too. We were not in Kansas anymore.

When we got to Manchester, we turned east again, and a little pee came out of me. "Uh.. say, Dad, where are we going?" I asked.

"Just up here a ways to the house we are flipping," he answered like it was nothing.

We turned north on Van Ness and then east on 80th something street and pulled up to a wreck of a house under remodeling. A temporary chain link fence surrounded it. We were deep in the hood. The only thing I knew about this area was what I saw on the news. The Watts riots were only a few years back, and I thought I could still smell the smoke. Dad pulled up, got out, and opened the padlock on the gate, and we drove in.

As El Jack pulled the cooler and some tools out of his van, Gabby and I stood at the fence and looked out into the neighborhood. Mostly, we were looking for what we expected to see. The houses were sunbaked, old bungalow style with bars on all the windows. Not every house, but a lot of them. There were black people hanging out on their front porches here and there. They were looking at us like, "What are you guys doing here?" We couldn't have been more out of place if we had been dolphins.

"Don't mind them," said El Jack, "you got every right to be here. You're helping to make this street better by making this house nicer. You leave them alone, and they will leave you alone."

"What if we don't want to leave them alone?" asked Gabby. "What if we want to talk to them?" Gabby always has to push it.

"Then, go ahead," said Dad. "They will respect you if you respect them. Hell, they might invite you to join the Crips. What black gang wouldn't want a couple of white boys to roll with them on their next drive by." Dad laughed, Gabby smiled. I didn't. I just shook my head and picked up a toolbox, and carried it into the house. That's Gabby. He is always drawn to strange places where he doesn't belong. That's why he's been able to tap into so many odd tribes around the world as an adult. Why he likes to hang out with a social cripple like me is a puzzle.

Dad pulled us together in the empty living room. The inside of the house was bare concrete. The walls were mostly stripped of drywall and freshly framed here and there with clean 2x4's to replace termite damage. All the doors were off, and the kitchen had no cabinets. Bits of wood, old drywall, and other construction garbage was all over the place. Dad gave us instructions.

"I want you guys to clean up this whole house. Put all the lumber pieces in a pile in the back yard according to size. Pieces bigger than 4 feet in one pile; small stuff in another. All the trash and broken drywall goes in the dumpster. Sweep out every room and clear the ground all around the house. If you get thirsty, the hose works. The toilet does too. There's a few lawn chairs out back under the tree when you want to take a break. Don't leave the property and keep the gate closed. There's no power, but I brought you a battery radio to keep you company. I'll be back at about 4 pm. Any questions?"

"You're leaving us here?" I asked.

"I've got another job to do. You'll be alright. Just don't leave the property. There is no store anywhere close that wasn't burned in the riot, so there's nowhere to go anyway. You've got your lunch. I'm leaving you a six-pack of cold RCs in the cooler. You've got all the tools you might need. Clean this joint up, and you'll get paid when I get back, OK?"

He wasn't asking because he didn't stay to hear me answer. He just turned, jumped in the van, and backed out. We closed the gate behind him as he drove off. We walked into the house and stood there looking at all the junk all over. It was overwhelming.

It was a little after 9 am. Gabby turned the radio on to KHJ, and we started working as Roy Orbison wailed 'Only the Lonely'.

To clear out the living room, Gabby stood near the sliding patio door, and I threw boards to him that he, in turn, threw outside in the general direction of the two piles. Soon, I was knocking the little pieces over with a longer 2x4 like a golfer, then batting them over baseball style. Gabby defended himself with a scrap of plywood. This made looking for small pieces I could smack at Gabby fun. Soon the living room was reasonably clear. Then we found it.

A lone golf ball. This was the original super-ball for us. It opened many possibilities. There were still lots of little blocks of 2x4 all around. We gathered a bunch and formed a whole baseball park that filled the empty living room floor. Gabby pitched the ball by rolling it down a ramp made from two boards nailed together. I batted it with a board on the ground rotated like a giant arcade game. Little blocks were set up all around the 'outfield'. What the ball hit determined if it was a single, double, triple, or out. If I hit the ball with the broken part of my 'bat', it would pop in the air. If Gabby caught it, I was out. If it got by him, it was a home run. We moved blocks of 2x4s around the bases as runners. The whole game was peppered with trash talk and improvised, vulgar play by play that would make Vin Scully blush. It was hysterical.

Before we knew it, it was 12noon, so we took a break for lunch. It was too hot to sit outside, so we brought the folding chairs inside to the cool of the concrete living room floor and ate our lunch. Munching on my most excellent sandwich, I looked around. We hadn't done much work yet, and we were halfway through the day. I had a slightly uneasy knot in my gut about it. We determined to get serious and drill in on the job.

After lunch, we broke down the baseball park and cleared out the inside of the house. I was sweeping the floor when the golf ball came bouncing off the wall at me. Of course, I blocked it with my broom and sent it back off the wall into the next room. Smack! Here it comes again! I had to do the splits like Rogie Vachon, the Kings goalie, to reach the 'puck,' but I blocked it from hitting my side of the house. I dropped the broom and picked up a 2x4, and brought the puck up the ice. Gabby checked me into the boards, and the puck went free. We locked in mortal combat to get possession and fire a slap shot bouncing off the concrete floors and ricocheting off the framing to score on the opposing wall. We called the play by play in our best Bob Miller voice. This game lasted until we broke a window.

While I swept up the glass, Gabby went outside to get the golf ball. When he didn't come back right away, I thought he couldn't find it, so I went out to help look. Gabby was standing in the yard, holding the ball. Facing him were four black guys on the other side of the fence. They were about our age, maybe a bit older and definitely more 'street'. There was one huge muscular guy with a giant Afro, a tall skinny guy in a Raiders hat, and two smaller dudes that had to be twins. They weren't smiling. Nobody was talking or moving. I walked up slowly and stood next to Gabby. I thought any second, guns were coming out, and we were done.

"Hey," I said as cheerful as I could.

Big Afro slowly swiveled his head and stared in silence. Then, the Skinny Raider spoke without hardly moving his lips. He said,

"What you doin on my street?"

"Working," answered Gabby.

"Don't sound like it. Y'all laughing and makin' noise."

"So?" Said Gabby.

I added, "Yeah, sorry about that; we've been goofing off playing hockey..."

Gabby cut me off with his hand.

"So what?" Gabby challenged, "we aren't bothering you. So what?"

Big Afro had a bulgy scar on his neck. Skinny Raider had a gold front tooth. They said nothing for a while, just staring us down. We didn't budge. Finally, Skinny Raider stepped out cocky as Flip Wilson and said,

"We want to play." Still, no smile.

Gabby looked him up and down. "You ever play ice hockey?"

"We're.. black... What do you think?"

"How do we know if you're any good?"

Big Afro leaned down and whispered something in Skinny's ear. Skinny translated. "He says, 'We all want to hit something with 2x4s. We'd rather it be that golf ball.'"

~ ~ ~

The score was tied at three. Gabby's team, Antoine (Big Afro) and Isaiah (one of the twins), had the puck. Gabby started from his own goal, the service bathroom, and brought it up through the kitchen. My team, Reggie (Skinny Raider) and Elisha (the other twin) were in a position to defend our goal, the back bedroom. Elisha checked Gabby but not before he passed the puck to Antoine through the hall. No one wanted the check the giant, but Reggie poked the golf ball out, and it went free towards me. I had my back to my goal, and I swatted the puck away. It went through the framing into the side bedroom where Isaiah was waiting. He knocked it back to Gabby, who had come through the living room to the edge of the hall. Gabby cocked and fired a slap shot off target, but the ball ricocheted off the wall and slid between my legs for a goal.

Gabby crowed like a rooster, Isaiah pumped his fist, and Antoine broke his 2x4 over his leg in celebration. Reggie slapped five to Gabby, and Elisha gave respect, laughing with everyone else. Just then, Charlie Tuna called the time on the radio at 3:30 pm. Oh, Crap.

"We got to get our work done quick," I said.

"What we got to do is get that goal back," objected Reggie.

"Got no more time. My Dad will be here any minute." No sooner than the words were spoken, I heard my Dad's van pulling up. I looked out the window and saw him opening the gate. "Crap! Help us clean this up!" I turned around to see our new friends disappearing over the back cinder wall faster than jackrabbits.

I swept up the glass and tried to finish the inside while Gabby ran around outside, trying to pick up trash, when my Dad rolled to a stop beside the dumpster. He got out and looked around. He didn't say anything, but his eyes said it all. He peeled a twenty out of his wallet and gave it to Gabby. Nothing for me. He just told us to get in, and we drove back to Torrance in silence. After he dropped off Gabby, he turned to me.

"What do you think about your work today?" He asked.

"I think I screwed up."

"What are you doing tomorrow?"

"Finishing the job?"

"Damn straight. Without Gabby."

I worked from 9 till 4 the next day, finishing all the cleaning, inside and out. I installed a new window and helped my Dad install new linoleum in the kitchen and bathroom. I caught sight of Reggie and Antoine outside the fence once, but they knew there was no fun in the house that day. At the end of the day, Dad gave me my $20.

"Sorry I screwed around yesterday," I confessed. "Don't blame Gabby; it was all my fault. You trusted me, and I goofed off."

"Well," he said, tussling my hair, "you can't put two young otters together and not expect them to play all day. I should have seen that coming. I'm glad you have a buddy. Next time, work first, play later."

El Jack was a man of few words. Those lessons I wear like a brand on my soul. (Still, to this day, Gabby and I can't get together without a circus breaking out). I had $45 in my pocket; tomorrow was Saturday, I had a date with destiny and, as they say, she just ordered the lobster...

Episode 6 - A Girl Gets in your Head

I got up in the middle of the night to pee. The bluish light of the television cast ghostly shadows into the hallway. Someone left it on last night. After finishing up in the bathroom, I stumbled into the den next to my bedroom to turn it off. -Click- The room went black, and a voice said, "What are you doing?"

The shock was so intense I wanted to jump out of my skin, but I was still mostly asleep, so I couldn't even find a scream. Instead, I just shook like jello and whimpered. When the adrenaline finally let go, I realized my sister Margie was sitting there in the dark, laughing at my jiggling panic. I tried to collect enough words to register a complaint, but they weren't at hand, so instead, I dropped into the sofa.

"Are you alright? You looked like you were having a stroke," she said, still chuckling. "Do you need a diaper change?"

"Shut up. You just scared me," I said. "What, what are you doing up so late?" I asked. The clock glowed 2 am. Margie sighed as the weight that had been crushing her settled back down again. The pale light barely showed her grey form in the recliner. Appropriate.

"Had a fight with Del. We broke up."

243

"I'm sorry. What happened?" I asked, not sure that I wanted to know.

She slowly shook her head. "I can't change who I am, and I sure as hell can't change him."

I didn't have an answer. She wasn't looking at me anyway, just staring into the space that used to hold her future.

"I guess it's better to find out now before you're married with kids," I offered.

"True. Hurts like hell, though." A few stray tears got out and wandered in the darkness.

"Was it worth it? You know, the pain and all. Is it worth trying?"

"Don't ask me that now. Maybe in a few days."

I tried to pull her away from her ache by being a little brother. "Tomorrow morning, I'm meeting Gabby and some friends, and there is a girl." it worked. Her head lifted, and she turned.

"Really? Does she like you?"

"I don't know, but I can't stop thinking about her."

"What's she like?"

"Beautiful. Athletic, but soft and funny.. and real smart. At least, I think she is. I guess I don't know too much about her yet, but I want to find out. I just hope she will want to find out about me, or it will get awkward."

"Don't be afraid of the awkward," said Margie, "It's always that way at first. It just makes the breakthrough that much sweeter when it happens. If it happens."

"What do you mean, 'breakthrough'? What's that?" I asked.

"It's the moment when both of you say 'No.'"

"No? Don't you mean 'yes'?

She slowly shook her head. "If she hasn't brushed you off, she's already said 'yes' to some extent. It's easy to say yes to a good time. Everybody's up for a party. The breakthrough comes when two lovers say 'No' to every other option. That moment will change your life."

"Didn't you have that with Del?"

"Del said 'yes' to me, but he never really said 'No' to his other options. He never will. I know that now but I let him use me for a long time, too long. Long after I said 'No' to MY other options. Do you understand?"

"I think so. Maybe." I turned this idea around like a skeleton key. She sensed my confusion.

"Well? Do you see other pretty girls at the beach?" she asked.

"Sure, lots of them."

"Would you trade any one of them for.. what's her name?"

"Jenny, it Jenny. And no, I don't think I would trade her for any other girl on the beach."

"Then, to some degree, you have already said 'no.' It's a 'no' to any other girl, but a 'yes' to Jenny. If she chooses you, then closes the door to any other guy, that's the breakthrough. That will blow your mind."

This idea was already blowing my mind. I was beginning to understand, but the more I did, the bigger the fear became.

"What happens if I say 'no' to all others, but she doesn't?"

"Then you will burn in hell. That's where I am right now."

I took three long breaths and let this all sink in. I've been standing on the edge of heartbreak and didn't even know it.

"Is it worth the risk?"

"No, but what else are we living for? Maybe you're too young to deal with love. Maybe you should stick to playing with your friends, reading your comic books, and watching 'Man from U.N.C.L.E.' On TV."

"I don't think I can go back."

"I know. Just be careful. Try to see past the frosting. Keep your No in your pocket until you find out more about this girl. Keep your relationship easy and light."

"What happens if we get the breakthrough?"

"That's when you will need to grow up real fast. It's not an easy thing to wear another person's devotion. It will take over your life. You can hurt each other badly. Are you ready for that? I think you have a simple and pure heart. Keep it that way. If you get it all beat up and broken before you're a full-grown man, you will never play your 'no' for anyone, even if you get married. You will be like Del. Or me. A bird with a broken wing."

"I hope you get another chance. Thanks for talking to me. I've got to go to bed."

I got up and hugged my big sister. As I left the room, the TV snapped on again. I closed my bedroom door and dreamed of being a kid without a care in the world.

~ ~ ~

I woke up early Saturday morning to the sound of my Dad getting ready for work. I asked him if I could catch a ride to his shop. He didn't ask me to work with him, but that was fine with me. Today I had to meet with the gang to finalize our plan to see the dead guy at Nu Pike. We were supposed to meet at the Horseshoe beach at 10. I could have made the hike down the Strand to Redondo, but I didn't want to be worn out when I got there. I wanted to look fresh, but not because there would be a beautiful girl there that I wanted to impress, just because.

I didn't dress in my usual white t-shirt and cutoffs. I put on a button-down paisley print shirt over my OP's. I was trying to kick it up a notch, again, for no particular reason. My Dad paused when he saw me.

"What are you dressed up for? Going to a funeral?"

"It's just a shirt. What's the big deal?" I deflected.

"I never see you wear a dress shirt in the summer. Meeting a girl?"

"Geeze! Can't a guy put on a shirt without a million questions?"

"Sure, but you want to iron that shirt first, you know, just in case a girl sees you."

"Why should I care if a girl sees me? Who am I? Bobby Sherman?"

"I guess not, but Bobby Sherman would iron that shirt before he put it on. Just in case, you know. And he would wear some cargo shorts over that bathing suit. Just saying."

"I'm just going to the beach. What's the big deal?"

"You need somewhere to keep all the money you're going to spend on her. No big deal. No skin off my nose. You're not dressing for me." Dad went into the bathroom to shave.

I ironed the shirt and put cargos on over my trunks. This was about as formal as a beach kid ever got unless he was on trial or was lying in a casket at his own funeral. I hoped it wasn't too much, too desperate. I hoped she would see that I was honoring her by presenting my best.

After worrying in the mirror for a bit, I went to the kitchen and poured a bowl of Cocoa Puffs. While I ate, a thought came to me. I tore a flap off the cereal box and wrote, 'NO' on it in big block letters with a pen. I folded it and put it in my front pocket. I felt a little more balanced.

I jumped in Dad's van, and we drove south down Valley, hung a right at Pier Ave, passed Either/Or Bookstore, and turned south on Hermosa Avenue. Dad dumped me out at Herdondo, and I walked past the marina to the Horseshoe. It was just past 9 am. I was early, so I got a cup of hot chocolate and sat on a bench overlooking the shore. The sand was deserted. The morning was chilly grey with morning clouds. Surfers in wet suits were taking advantage of the nice little break without bodies to dodge. I watched them cut and slash and make the most out of a five seconds. Then I saw her.

She wore an oversized cable knit sweater with a wide belt around the waist, Mod-like. Of course, I was already sold, so the cover-up just intensified my attraction. Sometimes there is more power in what is hidden than what is revealed. I saw her before she saw me. I watched her approach for a few seconds, and then she saw me, and a smile lit her face. Devastating. I wanted to jump into that warm sweater with her, but I held my ground and was thankful I had ironed my shirt.

"Hi, Chris," she chirped. "Are you the first one here?"

"Yeah, my Dad dropped me off on the way to work. I knew I would be early, but."

"Dave is getting some coffee. Can I sit with you?"

I just grinned stupidly and moved over. "How was your week?" she asked.

"Pretty good," I said. "Made some money. How about you?"

"I think we're all set. Pops gave us an advance on our allowance, so we're good."

"I scrounged around and did some chores for cash. Gabby and I worked for my Dad."

"Well, you made enough to get a decent shirt, I see." She nodded her approval. (Hmm.. why did that sting just a little?)

Dave walked up with two cups of coffee. Gabby and Roxanne were in tow. Jenny took her coffee and cradled it with two hands, like you see in a commercial.

"Lawler, what the hell?" said Dave. "Gabby says you were almost shot in the hood last week. Says he saved your life and became king of the Crips."

"Yeah, I happened just like that," I said, winking at Gabby. "He's a real homie now."

Just then, Carl walked up. He didn't wait to greet everyone. He was bursting with news.

"Listen, you guys," he started. "You know how I told you about my brother's friend who works at the Pike? Randy is picking him up after his shift tonight, and they are going to a party in Long Beach. He said he would take us all in the back of his pickup. My brother said his friend would let us in the employee entrance at 5 pm. Then Randy will pick us up at 11 pm on his way home. We'll have a ride there and back AND get in free to boot. But, it's got to be tonight. What do you think?"

"Does everyone have cash?" asked Gabby. Everyone nodded except Roxanne.

"Getting in free helps, but I'm pretty light for anything else," she said.

"Don't worry about it," said Carl. "I'll buy you a hot dog and a coke."

She was surprised by Carl's offer. We all were. We all knew she had a thing for Carl. Good for her.

"I haven't asked my parents yet," I said. "I didn't think it would happen so soon."

"What about the rest of you?" asked Carl. He was really pushing to make this happen.

"I think we can go, right?" said Jenny, looking at her brother.

"I think so," said Dave. "They trust us. I think we can get permission."

Gabby said, "I'm good to go. My parents are out at the lodge tonight. They won't be home until 2 am."

"I think I can go if YOU are asking me," said Roxanne, looking at Carl.

"What? Like a date?" asked Carl.

"My Dad will let me go if I'm going to be with someone, not just in a mob."

"Ok, Sure." Carl squared up to Roxanne. "Roxy, will you go out with me tonight to Nu Pike?"

"I'd love to. It's a date."

What? Just like that, those two were an item? I was amazed. Is that the way it's done? Roxanne glowed with new joy. Carl acted like he just scratched his elbow. Jenny clapped for her girlfriend and finished with a quick glance at me. I wasn't sure what that meant, but I noticed Carl looking at Jenny instead of Roxy. Hmm...

"Excellent," said Carl. We're all set."

"Except for Chris," added Roxanne.

"Well, get it done, Lawler. We can't go without you, can we?" said Carl, with the warmth of a snake. "Be at my house ready to go at 4 pm. We can't wait if you're late, so be on time or stay home. Got it?" Everyone agreed.

"So what are we doing for the rest of the day?" asked Roxanne. "It doesn't look like any of us is ready for the beach."

"Yeah, too cold," said Jenny. "Why don't we all go to our house and hang out, maybe play some pool?"

"I'm cool with that," said Carl. "Puts us close to my house. Got any beer in the fridge of your den?"

"Sure," answered Dave, "every bottle named and numbered by my Dad. Don't expect a party."

"We don't need it to have some fun," declared Jenny. Let's just hang out and play some records. My Mom will probably make us some lunch."

"Where do you guys live?" I asked her.

"Avenue D, off Prospect. Carl's house is near Rat Beach, just south of the Riviera. We can walk down the Strand to Esplanade. It's a pretty walk on the bluff. Want to go?"

Everyone was willing. I was torn. Permission for Nu Pike was probably back at my house in Manhattan Beach. Honestly, I thought if I left the group now, I probably wouldn't see them again, and I'd be stuck home while they went to the Pike. I didn't think my Mom would agree to let me go, so why waste the whole day trying? Here, at least I had a chance to hang out with

Jenny and the rest of Gabby's gang for a day. I was about to surrender to defeat when a thought hit me.

"My Dad's shop is on PCH south of Knob Hill. He might be there, and I can ask about tonight. If not, I'll have to go back home. Can we stop by on the way?"

"Sure, we can do that, right?" asked Jenny, not really looking for an answer. Everyone agreed. We picked up and moved out.

We walked along the parking bluff that skirted Veterans Park. The clouds were just starting to break some. It was probably going to be a spectacular beach day eventually, but when you live at the beach, you can shamelessly waste days like this. I didn't care; my mind was on other things.

So there are six of us walking along the sidewalk overlooking one of the most beautiful beaches in the world. We can't move along like an unorganized mob. Some marching order was trying to assert itself awkwardly. Normally, I'd be hoofing alongside Gabby. But Gabby was talking to Dave. Roxanne kept pace with her new 'other,' Carl, but Carl was edging back to be closer to Jenny. I'm thinking, 'what the hell, man? Walk with your date and get out of my space! I pushed up next to her and tried to act like I didn't care. She acknowledged me with a little smile but also looked at Carl. Confusing.

"Have you always lived in Redondo?" I asked her.

"We were born here, lived in our house forever. I'm about as local as it gets. How about you? We're you born in Manhattan Beach?" She said 'Manhattan' with awe like it was Beverly Hills.

"No, I just moved there last year from Bay Village in Torrance. That's where Gabby and I became friends. Before that, I grew up in the Valley in Lake View Terrace." A little air came out of her balloon.

"Oh... the Valley? Isn't it pretty hot out there?"

I squirmed just a beat. Then I decided to own it. "Yep, like the surface of hell. And we didn't have a beach. I had a garden hose and a drainage pit called Hansen Dam. You grew up with dolphins. I grew up with skunks and coyotes." She laughed at my honesty. Good sign. Cracked the ice a little.

Jenny told me about her family and elementary school and other stuff, but I admit, I wasn't paying a lot of attention. I was distracted by Carl trying to ignore Roxanne's attention while doing his best to interject smart ass jokes into our conversation. I felt bad for Roxy. It's like she got an ice cream cone, but it was melting in her hand. She deserved better.

We made a turn inland at Knob Hill and then south on PCH. A block and a half brought us to my Dad's shop, Gardena Floor Covering. The gang waited out front as I went in.

There was no one in the showroom, and El Jack was sitting behind his desk with a phone in hand. He was locked in a heated conversation with my Mom. Sounded ugly. I wanted to minimize my time there, so I stood in front of his desk and tried to interrupt. He kept brushing me off, but I kept pestering until he finally put a hand over the phone and whispered, "WHAT!!?"

I could hear Mom still ranting on the phone, oblivious that she was being ignored for the moment. I fired my request like a machine gun.

"My-friends-are-going-to-Long-Beach-to-the-Pike-tonight-and-I-really want-to-go-and-I-have-money-and-I'll-be-back-about-12-and-they-are-all-waiting-for-me-so-can-I-go? Please? PLEASE?

He was trying to listen to my Mom with one ear and me with the other, so I think all he got from me was, "Can I go to the beach with my friends till 12?" He gave me the 'whatever' look and waved me off. I knew he didn't hear me, but I took that nod as complete agreement and split before he could think about it. Did I feel bad about it? Hell, no. He's the one who told me that it's easier to ask for forgiveness than permission. His nod gave me a get-out-of-jail card if things went south when I got back.

"I'm good to go," I announced to the gang as I left the shop. Everyone cheered but Carl. I hushed and hustled them away from the scene of my crime.

Dave and Jenny's house was an immaculate tribute to suburban mid-century design. Not that I knew what that was at the time, it just seemed like the kind of house James Bond would live in if he retired to Redondo. Jenny's Mom, Janice West, was a beautiful older version of Jenny. She wore a left-handed smile over soft freckles that set her eyes laughing. Her fully developed figure doubled the bounty on her daughter. Where Jenny leaned a little to the hippy style, her Mom was Sinatra Swank. Tailored blouse, smart hip-hugging pants, and a 'That Girl' flip of her burnished copper hair were all business. No lazy homemaker here. She set a high bar for her daughter. She greeted us at the door and ushered us safely through her showcase home into a spacious den. All of Gabby's gang had been here before, and they fell right into the array of amusements while 'Janice' (she wouldn't let us call her 'Mrs. West') went to work making lunch.

Dave and Gabby grabbed pool cues and racked up a game. Carl went to work on a Monkees themed pinball machine. Roxanne watched him dutifully. Jenny poured over an extensive record collection and set up some to cycle through her parent's Magnavox console. First up to be kissed by the snakehead stylus was the Grass Roots' "Midnight Confession." Not exactly cutting edge but a safe choice for a curated teenage soda pop party. Then it was the Monkees, Herman's Hermits, and Peggy Lee while Jenny's Mom served tomato soup and grilled cheese sandwiches. After Janice retired to the living room for soap operas, I noticed the music took a more provocative turn. The 'Rubber Soul' Beatles, the Animals, and Stones pumped a darker vibe into the room.

While the pool table was occupied, I gravitated to a cabinet full of darts. These were not the kind of plastic darts I knew as a kid; they were finely crafted, weighted, and balanced works of art that were sensual to throw. They pierced the vintage bristle board with a whisper of 'thunk.' I threw a few because it felt so good, but I was not very good at it. Thankfully, the corkboard surrounded the target.

"You're not so bad, but you could be better," said Jenny from behind me. She surprised me in mid-stroke, and the dart caught the wall just outside the cork.

"Oh, my God, I'm sorry," I said sheepishly.

"Don't worry. If you could see what's on the other side of that cork, you would know there are no pros around here. My Dad and his friends have filled that wall with so many holes; an Irish pub would be proud. If you want to hit the target, you would have to stop strangling the dart. Let me show you."

She picked up three darts and held two in her left hand and one between her fingers of her right. "You have to hold the other two in your hand to feel balanced. Hold the one you will toss as light as a butterfly. Turn your shoulder sideways, so the bend of your arm is straight up and down. One, two, three, release!" The dart flew in a graceful arc and thunked just below the bullseye.

I tried to replicate her delivery, but it felt awkward. My dart hit the board out of the scoring circle.

"Try again," she said. I took my stance, and she used her hands to correct my feet, straighten my back, and tuck my elbow in. She even brushed my Bobby Sherman flip of hair out of my eye. So much touching from this girl was like being electrocuted with joy. She folded her body against mine and held my throwing hand. She smelled like a garden after the rain. We moved together, one, two, three, and released the dart. Double seventeen. I turned my head to smile, and her face was right.. there.. just like I was in a movie.

"Move over," said Carl, "I'll show you how it's done." He pissed on the spark before it caught fire and then showed me up by sinking two darts in the center circle, one in the bullseye. "That's the money," he crowed. He then ignored me and turned to Jenny.

"You're a good teacher. How about I teach you a lesson? How about best of five Cricket?"

"English or American?" answered Jenny.

"English, of course," replied Carl, retrieving his darts. With that, they were off in a rollicking trash-talking contest that I had no part in.

The pool game was still occupied. I wandered to the sofa where Roxanne was sitting alone watching a "Chiller" feature on TV.

"Mind if I watch with you?" I asked, sitting down.

"Sure," she said flatly.

I watched in silence for a little. "It, The Terror From Outer Space" was on. This movie really scared me as a kid. Something out the monster's brutal thrashing and how the astronaut gets trapped in the room with it. It was unnerving. Roxanne was completely shut down. When a commercial came on, a ventured a word.

"Not working out?" I said quietly. I nodded in the direction of Carl and Jenny, laughing over their game.

"Oh, it's working out just the way it always works out. Jenny is my best friend, but she is a black hole for guy's attention."

"How do you know what a black hole is?" I asked. Astronomer John Wheeler just coined that term this year for an object of such intense gravity, nothing escaped, even light. "How did you know that?"

She thumbed herself, saying, "Science nerd." She thumbed at Jenny and said, "Black Hole." She crossed her arms. "You should know, you're caught in her gravitational field. So is Carl. The difference is, your falling for her, but he's diving after her."

I was shocked that she could read my mail so easily. "Man, it's been a crazy day for you. Highs and lows."

"That's what happens to a booster. You lift off with a bang, then drop back to earth after you deliver your payload. I delivered Carl to Jenny, and now I'm dropping." There were no tears, just a simmering resolution.

"How do you know about rocket...?"

"...Boosters? I told you, science nerd. Try to keep up."

His cockiness made me laugh then she laughed too. She touched my arm. "Sorry. It's not you; it's just my life." She turned her attention back to the TV. 'IT' was gutting some poor Kawalski. The little boy in me shuddered.

"Gabby and I are rocket freaks. We buy Estes rockets and then modify them with fireworks to do wicked things that would make Mr. Estes cry."

Roxy's eyes lit up. "Tell me about it."

I lost track of time as we watched 'It' die in space, talked about the Apollo missions, laser technology, and the brand new IBM computer that was so compact that it only filled one room. We laughed at Chiller's second feature, 'Attack of the Killer Tomatoes.' At one point, Jenny came and sat on the other side of me. She tried to dial into our conversation, forcing me to whip my head back and forth between them. I broke that paradox by getting up to use the bathroom. When I came out, everyone was getting ready to move on to Carl's house.

We left Jenny and Dave's house and walked to the Riviera. Just south of the charming little shops was a residential neighborhood between Palos Verdes Blvd. and Rat (Right After Torrance) Beach. We came to a house that stuck out from the rest because it had zero warmth. Carl lived there with his single father and older brother. There was no woman to touch the place with grace. Carl didn't even let us inside. He just went in and yelled for his brother Randy while we all piled into the back of Randy's '62 Chevy C10. It was a tight fit, but I didn't complain; I was pressed up against Jenny. Carl jammed in on her other side. Randy came out smoking a cigarette, looking like a redneck, and said nothing but, "Hold on". We took off for a night that none of us will ever forget.

Episode 7 - The Pike

We were all piled into the back bed of a hopped-up '62 Chevy C10 pickup truck. We sat freely on the rusty deck with no restraints at all. Randy, Carl's older brother, did not drive like he held the tender lives and bright futures of six young teenagers in his hands. He drove like a moonshiner with a load of potatoes for the still. '56 Rockabilly Elvis blared out of his eight-track, declaring we were going to be "A-Rockin Tonight." Randy sang along with no shame as he ground through the gears trying to burn rubber. We loved it.

To get to Long Beach without drawing too much attention from the cops, he avoided PCH and instead drove East on Palos Verdes Drive North. It wound through the boondocks of Rolling Hills past mini ranches and horse property. We rumbled along in the back, squashing to one side, then the other as Randy took the curves with a squeal of rubber. I can tell you; I did not mind at all being pressed into Jenny in ways that would make her slap my blushing face any other time. We all got real familiar.

When we drove past Western and came to the five corner intersection where Anaheim Street would have taken us straight into Long Beach, Randy yelled from inside, "You want the Bridge?" We answered in unison, "To the Bridge!" Randy turned south on Gaffey, and we dropped towards San Pedro.

Before he got to the road that would commit us to the Vincent Thomas Bridge, he pulled into a liquor store. We took that moment to straighten our clothes and smooth our hair.

"Your brother is crazy," said Dave, laughing.

Gabby added, "I don't think there will be anything at the Pike to match this ride."

Randy came out of the liquor store with two sacks. He took a pull on a bottle wrapped in one sack and gave the other to Carl. While Randy changed the eight-track to a classic Gene Vincent cassette, Carl passed an open bottle of something in the bag. Ugh, this night was taking a turn.

My mom was a hopeless alcoholic. Growing up with this in my family pretty much killed the charm of drinking for me. Frankly, I hated that crap for what it did in my house. Nobody knew that about me, except Gabby, so I balked when the bottle came to me. Jenny had taken a pull, coughed, then laughed and passed it to me. The pressure was so intense. Am I with her or not? I did not want to be 'that guy.' I admit I didn't have balls big enough to stand against the tide. So, I took the bottle and pressed it against my closed lips, and faked it. I passed it on to Roxanne, and she held up a palm.

"Not for me."

"C'mon, Roxy, loosen up," said Carl, shaming her.

"Don't want it. Don't need it. Pass." She didn't refuse with judgment or a superior attitude. She didn't even break her smile.

She just held HER ground. I was impressed. I got schooled. After her refusal, the bottle came to Gabby, and he passed too. Dave didn't. I felt ashamed for even faking it. The bottle passed on, and Carl doubled down, and so did the twins. Awkward. What's worse, I noticed Randy sucking his bottle down while he drove.

When we got in line for the toll booth, Randy told us to lay down. He didn't want any attention. We squashed down in the bed as far as we could get and kept quiet until the toll was paid, and we began to rise into the late afternoon sky. The view of the harbor from the apex of the bridge was amazing. We all cranked around to look at the ships below. The roller coaster at the Pike was just visible in the distance. While we strained to see all we could, Jenny's hand found mine, and without looking at me, she closed her fingers around it. I guess she was loosening up. That moment was a slug of moonshine to me. My ride was just beginning.

We cruised into Long Beach with "Be Bop a Lula," opening the door to a new world. This city looked like it would be more at home in New Jersey than California. I wondered if this was like the Bronx in New York. Definitely a tougher, gritty vibe. The South Bay is full of mostly bedroom communities that cradle a population that works elsewhere. Long Beach is home to the Navy and longshoremen working the docks where the world's products come to America. It's a shore leave town full of rowdy bars, fish markets, and rent by the hour flops houses where sailors try to shed their sea legs. There is no beautiful shoreline full of bikini girls and sun-bleached surfers. The Red Line terminated there, bringing inner city folks to the docks for work. And the Pike.

With the city to our left, we turned right down an incline into the Fun Zone. We drove around the big lot and past a sign that marked the employee parking. Randy pulled up right in front of the gate that said, "Employees Only." We climbed out of the truck bed and straightened out while Randy ran inside to get his friend. He came back with a skinny greaser dude who looked us over and rolled his eyes. He held the gate open, and we went in. Randy yelled after us, "Pick you up here at eleven. Don't be late." He didn't wait for an answer; he and the Greaser were gone just like that.

We walked around the seedy offices and backstage area where supplies were piled up, and broken junk littered the alley. We saw a pile of knock off stuffed Disney characters dumped outside what must have been a carnival game. What's trash in the ally is a grand prize on the Midway. At last, we came to a break in the buildings where we saw a Gypsy looking woman walking through, and we followed her. Once through the gap, we stepped back into time.

This could have been the Atlantic City Boardwalk for all its back east charm. The noise, the crowd, and the faintly decaying smell seemed to capture the seedy spirit of Coney Island. We just stood there in the middle of the Midway, taking it in. The sound was like a riot of little bits of music, bells, pneumatic blasts of compressed air, screaming little kids, and murmuring crowd noise. Carneys barked at us to come to play their sucker games. I half expected to see Mafia boss Carlo Gambino come strolling down the walk with a doll on his arm and a squad of Zoot suited goombahs in his wake. Jenny grabbed my hand and said, "Let's try the horse race!" The sensory overload and her claiming touch made me oblivious to the two characters that followed us out from the employee area.

We squirted our way to a cheap, stuffed Goofy that probably cost a nickel to make in Mexico but extracted $2 bucks from me to 'win.' I presented it to Jenny in triumph. She accepted it and turned around to give it to a little kid walking by. (Hey, that's two bucks of charity you're giving away). Oh well, easy come, easy go.

Next, Gabby and I got into a duel with the BB machine guns, trying to shoot the star on the target entirely off. It was about impossible, of course, but the fun of emptying a full clip like a gangsta was rewarding enough. I bought myself a salted pretzel and offered Jenny a bite. She refused but asked me for a pile of chicken wings (three times the price), and I coughed up the cash. She ate two and gave the rest to Dave. After we ate, I took our wrappers to a trash can with an elephant head top, and the papers were sucked out of my hand into its mouth with a vacuum. It made throwing your trash in the can fun. I guess that's what they had in mind. I kinda felt like that was happening to my cash too.

We worked our way through the Midway, playing some games and pausing to watch a sailor get a tattoo. The guy doing the tattoo was almost completely covered with art. The sailor was getting a girl's name tattooed inside a heart with an arrow through it. I commented, "What if he breaks up with that girl? Will he have to find a new girlfriend with the same name?"

Dave said, "He will just cross that one out and tat the new name below."

Carl added, "Yeah, sort of like adding notches in his belt. It shows what a Casanova he is."

Gabby noted, "It would be more practical to get a big heart on his arm and tattoo: 'Your Name Here' in it." Brilliant.

We laughed pretty hard at that joke, and I don't think the sailor was too happy about it on the other side of the glass.

"We better move on before that guy is finished," I said. "I don't think he likes being the butt of our joke." Everyone noticed the guy glaring at us, and we got the hell out of there.

Down the way, we heard a band playing from inside the Lido Ballroom. It was a cover band playing Monkees hits along with surf rock and other top forty hits. The Cyclone Racer demon coaster was looming in the distance, and the guys wanted to get on mission and do what we came here for, but we were overruled. The girls wanted to check out the band and see if there was dancing. Jenny grabbed my hand again and pulled me in.

Now, I wasn't exactly 'with' Jenny yet, but she was sorta treating me like it. With no official declaration or bang of a gong or blast from a train whistle to mark the turn in our relationship, I was left excited but confused. I didn't plan on being in such a passive role, but I could not get ahead of her. She was aggressive and decisive in a way that I hadn't developed yet. She pulled me right onto the dance floor and started 'jerking' and 'swimming' and doing all kinds of dances that I never heard of. She was a terrific dancer and worth watching if only I didn't have to try and keep up. I have never been a dancer. I became a drummer so I could hide from the dance floor. I moved with clumsy imitations of what she did as best I could. Watching Jenny's body move with sensual authority was hypnotizing. I didn't even notice Carl dancing right next to me. Jenny turned slightly to release me and dance with Carl. I faded off the dance floor and watched them.

"Got kicked, huh?" said Roxanne.

"I guess. I'm not much of a dancer."

"Me too, I mean, me neither,' Roxy said." I think I'm too big. I sort of lumber more than dance."

The next song played was a hard-driving version of 'Wipe Out.' Carl and Jenny killed it. While they were stealing the thunder, I looked around for the others.

"Where's Dave and Gabby?" I asked.

"Dave is in front of the bandstand, and Gabby is over there." She pointed to the left of Carl. Gabby had found a strange girl and was lost in abandon. I think he is the first guy to dance like nobody's looking. I wish I had that freedom. I looked at Roxanne, bopping her head slightly to the beat.

"You want to, you know, dance?" I offered.

She looked at me sideways for a second, then said, "Sure, ok."

She let the bop in her head spill to the rest of her body, and she moved out on the floor with a safe, contained rhythm. I followed her, doing just enough to qualify as dancing. It was easy and comfortable. Then, like ten seconds later, the song was over. Before the dance floor cleared, the band dropped seamlessly into the Beach Boy's, "Surfer Girl." We could have abandoned the floor like Carl and Jenny did, but we didn't. We drew together and rocked ever so gently to the slow groove. At first, we were arm's length. As the groove settled in, we drew closer until I held her to me. Instead of rocking back and forth the way preteens will do, Roxy eased into a 'one-and-a, two-and-a' rhythm almost like a waltz. She pulled me in with just the slightest pressure that said to me, "c'mon, you know? I need a break." She was used to being disappointed, but her gentle need exposed a gift I could choose to give her. I pulled her waist in and folded my arms around her. She laid her head on my shoulder, and for just a few minutes, we belonged to each other. I purposely avoided looking into her eyes, and she did not seek mine. With this single restraint, we preserved plausible deniability. The music ended, and we broke our embrace and walked off the dance floor past Jenny with her jaw hanging loose.

"What was that?" she asked,

"I know. I'm not a very good dancer," I replied. Jenny narrowed her gaze at me, but I just maintained my innocent 'Alfred E. Neumann' face. Plausible Deniability.

Jenny grabbed my hand firmly and almost jerked me beside her. As we walked out of the Lido, I caught a glance from Roxanne with just the hint of a left-handed smile on her lips. What I missed was seeing the same two guys that followed us in through the employee entrance follow us out of the Lido.

Along the Midway, we got lost in the House of Mirrors, raced through the FunHouse, and got sick on the Tilt-a-Whirl. All the while, Jenny kept an eye on me, Carl hovered close by, and Roxanne shot little smirks my way, letting me know she was enjoying the show. Besides that silly preteen intrigue, we were just kids having a blast.

We took a break to get some food. I got a hotdog, and I bought Jenny (you guessed it) a steak sandwich. It was way better than that Jack in the Box version and way more expensive. And, it didn't come with any vulgar humor potential. Even though I wasn't on an official date with Jenny, she was comfortable running through my money as if she owned me. Meanwhile, I noticed that true to his word, Carl bought Roxanne a hotdog and Coke, then proceeded to sit next to Jenny to eat his double cheeseburger. He got wrapped up in a conversation with Jenny while I watched Roxanne, watching a mom trying to corral her kids out on the Midway.

Roxy didn't have the classic female beauty lines that Jenny had, but I decided that was ok. Her face was kind, and her smile was warm. Roxy didn't have the classic surfer girl hair like Jenny, but that was ok too. She was just a bit tall, and her body wasn't intensely sculpted the way Jenny kept hers.. and that was ok. In fact, every time I noticed something about Roxanne that wasn't as perfect as Jenny but gave it a pass, I felt a greater attachment to the nerd girl. What the hell is happening?

'We've been avoiding it for too long," said Gabby. "Let's do what we came here to do. The rides are that way."

We wrapped up our trash, fed it to the sucking Gorilla trash can, and walked on through the crowd towards the ride section. Along the way, we heard mechanical laughing. It was coming from the Laff in the Dark ride. Two mechanical dummies that must have been there since the Civil War rocked and jerked in fake hysterics that were just plain creepy. This is where the dead guy is supposed to be on display.

Dave said, "It's right here. Let's get it over with."

"No, not yet," said Carl. "I want to see where he was killed first. Let's see if his blood is still up there." He thumbed towards the Cyclone Racer.

"I don't know," hedged Roxanne. "That thing looks pretty intense. Maybe I'll take a pass and wait for you guys here."

"No way, Rox," said Carl. "We are all in this together. All for one, one for all." (Huh? When did we say that?)

Dave seconded Carl's objection. "We have to stick together. We can warm up to the Cyclone with this." He pointed at a smaller roller coaster called the "Wilde Maus." Peer pressure prevailed, and she reluctantly got in line for the smaller coaster.

Most of the rides so far looked like they were County Fair standards. The Wilde Maus (what? Carneys don't know how to spell?) was a rusty two-person coaster with switchbacks on top and a few little drops here and there. It had that 'get to the point' metal scaffolding structure that didn't waste a dime on charm. When we got to the front of the line, Jenny made sure I was with her in our car. Then came Gabby and Roxy, then Carl and Dave.

The ride was violent. The drops were not just gravity falls but seemed to be throwdowns. The top switchbacks on top were angry, bone wracking whiplash turns that wiped the smile off your face. When it was over, I was glad to get out of that thing. So was Jenny.

"That was fun," said Gabby, rubbing his neck.

"I think I lost a filling," said Roxy.

When Carl and Dave got out of their car, they were laughing like they just cheated death.

"That top switchback section was brutal," said Dave.

"If you have squished into me any harder, I would be pregnant now," said Carl.

Roxanne tried to finger brush her hair back in shape. "Well, I don't know if that qualifies as getting ready for the Cyclone, but I need a minute before we go on. I'm going to sit down over there." She pointed at a bench, and we all thought it was a great idea.

As we sat there trying to realign our backs, Carl went to get something from a shop. He came back with a little bag of saltwater taffy. He offered it around.

"Have one," insisted Carl. "These will settle your stomach." Everyone took one, and Jenny took two. She unwrapped one and fed it to me. It seemed odd, but I ate it. I noticed that there were only enough for all of us to have one each. Hmm...

Episode 8 - The Cyclone Racer

As we sauntered to the Cyclone Racer, Gabby came up to me and whispered, "You didn't eat that taffy, did you?"

"Yes, didn't you?" I asked.

He responded by showing me his taffy still wrapped in a twist of pink paper. "I think Carl spiked them with something. You better watch yourself."

"How do I do that? Watch myself?" I whispered.

"If you start to feel strange, lock onto me. I'll keep you in touch with reality."

"What are you two whispering about?" asked Roxanne, entering our hushed conversation.

"Did you eat the taffy?" I asked her.

"Hell no, I've known Carl for too long." She showed her wrapped taffy still in her palm.

"Crap! Why didn't you guys tell me?"

"Just be cool, man," assured Gabby. "It's probably nothing to worry about. If things get weird, we'll get you through it."

"It's already weird." I looked at Carl. He was lost in a conversation with Jenny about whether the Monkees are a real band or not. Jenny ate her taffy and made sure that I ate mine. Did she know? Of course.

We approached the Cyclone Racer. The wooden coaster was ancient and smelled like the Redondo pier on a hot day when the tar is soft. It was a twin-track monster of a ride that squeezed screams out of girls and cussing out of guys. The constant sound of fear mixed with the growl of the cars straining against the tracks left no doubt about its purpose. It was designed and built by rowdy roughnecks of a different era who were probably dead and in torment for their sins by now. Gabby and I looked at each other like wolves about to feed. This was our kind of ride.

The sun had set, and the little lights that outlined the swooping curves and plummeting drops of the coaster's path implied a false sense of innocence. Music blared from a PA near the entrance. It was Steppenwolf's "Born to be Wild". The line was pretty long, being the premier ride at the Pike. We had to walk back the way we came to find the end of it. The line fed into a slow moving switchback section set aside to keep it from snaking all the way through the park.

"So Carl," asked Dave, pitching him a softball, "exactly where did the kid get his head cut off?" Carl stepped out a little to 'take the stage' and spoke up so everyone around us could hear.

"They say the chop happened on the second hump after the cyclone section. The right side car was at maximum speed, zooming a little bit ahead of its twin car on the left, when a kid stood up to show off to his date beside him and his friends in the other car. He turned backwards to gloat, and when they came to the top of the second hill, he never saw the sign that says, "DANGER - DO NOT STAND". A support beam caught him just right and knocked his head off like it was a little league t-ball. His blood squirting body fell back over his date. His head fell in the lap of his older brother in the left car. It was still laughing and grinning."

Everyone that heard him winced at the gore. I think a few people even changed their minds about riding and left the line. Carl just laughed. He was soo pleased with himself. Gabby and I were laughing. We had to give him points for storytelling.

"That's hideous," said Roxanne. "You're making little kids cry."

Dave put his hand up. "One question, did he get a refund?" Snickers.

Gabby answered, "Probably half off his next visit." Nothing like gallows humor.

"So where is the bloodstain they could not clean?" Asked Jenny.

Carl answered, "The kid's body flipped around in the throes of death and hosed the track with his blood all along the second drop on the right side. We have to ride the right side coaster to see it. I've heard that part of the track is haunted."

"Seriously? sneered Dave. "Haunted by the headless ghost of a show-off?"

"No. It was haunted before that kid was killed. That guy is not the only person murdered by this ride."

After that, no one talked for a while. We inched along and entered the switchback section. The line narrowed to single file. Carl nosed between Jenny and I and got her and Dave talking about Redondo Union High School, where they were headed in the fall. I was going to Mira Costa, so I had no part in their discussion. The line crept forward, and I fell back next to Roxy and Gabby.

"Five," I said to Gabby and Roxanne.

"Five what?" said Roxy. Gabby knew what I meant. He let me set it up.

"The fifth guy that passes you coming the other way in this switchback will be your husband." Roxanne gave me a puzzled look. Gabby counted off the men that passed her until the fifth one appeared. It was an older grandpa with his grandson.

"There he is," said Gabby, "I hope he remembers his heart pills on your honeymoon." Roxanne laughed.

"Oh, I get it. Funny. Alright, Seventh girl to pass will be your date to your senior prom."

"Whose?" I asked.

"Both of you will have to fight for her."

We passed a few pretty girls, and then the seventh came into view. She was a big Mexican cholo girl with tattoos on her massive arms. We all chuckled. The cholo gave us a stabbing look, and we zipped up our lips and looked at the ground until she passed down the line.

Gabby asked, "Did you say fight over her or with her? I think she would kill us both."

"Alright, this one's for you, Gab," I said. "You have to touch and speak to the tenth girl that passes us."

"Pffft, no problem," said Gabby. Several little kids went by, three of the girls. Any female is in play, but Gabby didn't want to accost a little girl and get punched by their Dad. Then came an older lady, then two Chinese girls. Finally, the tenth girl appeared. She was still down the line, but she was gorgeous and hanging on her boyfriend's arm. How was he going to play it?

The couple inched by, and Gabby reached out and touched her arm, saying, "Excuse me, are you the ones that won the dance contest at the Lido tonight?" They were both flattered by the compliment but said no.

"Smooth move," said Roxanne. "Using flattery to touch another guy's date. Too easy."

"Ok, Roxy," said Gabby. "Show us how it's done. The seventeenth guy you pass in line, you have to reach out, grab his face in both your hands and kiss him on the lips."

She giggled at that but refused, saying, "No way, Jose. I'm not going to make out with a total stranger."

"Alright, but you have to at least touch his hair. That's fair, right?" Gabby consulted with me to get a ruling. I agreed.

Roxanne rolled her eyes. "Ok, fine."

We watched the line to see who it would be. First to pass were a gang of high school jocks in their Narbonne High School letterman jackets. Then came a tall skinny guy and two fat biker dudes that passed by to her relief. Next came five Boy Scouts in uniform. Gabby asked one of them, "What kind of a merit badge do you get for making out with a strange girl?" They all went, "eeuww!"

Five dudes to go as we neared the end of a switchback. At the same time, we all counted ahead the remaining guys to pass and realized the seventeenth guy would be ME as I turned the corner. A shower of embarrassment washed over me. For a second, I thought of at least switching my place in line with Gabby, but he would have none of it. Gabby counted the last few guys out loud.

"15, 16, SEVENTEEN," he said with authority, pointing at me and grinning like a Cheshire Cat.

"Oh, crap," I said.

Roxanne was blushing. Then she said, "Screw it." She reached out with two hands and grabbed my head with no doubt, and kissed me full on the lips. Hard and long. She released my face gently, with just a little lingering look, brushing the hair out of my eyes, then stared straight ahead. Gabby stood there with his mouth open for a beat, then cracked up. I was stunned. Right there, right then, that girl put an impure thought in my mind. The Classics IV's "Spooky" was playing on the PA overhead. Can't hear that song to this day without goosebumps about a dark-haired, 13-year-old nerd girl.

I played it cool. Gabby laughed so hard that it made Carl, Dave, and Jenny turn around to see what was happening.

"What's so funny?" asked Carl.

"Nothing," said Gabby, still chuckling. "You had to be there."

Jenny eyeballed me up and down. The tumblers were rolling around inside her head with nothing to lock onto. She turned back around suspiciously and rebooted the conversation with Dave and Carl, but not before giving me one more 'WTF' glance over her shoulder.

I quietly looked at Roxanne. Someone had insisted that her curly hair be cut in a shoulder-length Barbara Streisand bob, but that wild mane had other ideas. Laughing curls rebelled this way and that but only made me want to join the rebellion. Funny, until then, I never noticed her hair before. She kept her eyes forward except for a small glance, punctuated with that little left-handed smile.

Gabby came alongside me. "Your eyes are glassy. How are you feeling? Anything strange going on?"

"Besides that?" I nodded in Roxy's direction. "I don't feel high or sped up if that's what you mean. I'm alright." As soon as those words left my lips, I noted just the slightest rise in the intensity of color. It might just be my imagination, or looking too hard for some high effect, or, maybe, it was Roxanne's kiss. I couldn't tell, but I had a whole new load on my mind to think about.

Finally, we came to a split in the line that would divert the riders to the left or right tracks. We fell into the right-hand side. Then we had a choice to make. Sit anywhere, or go for the front car. We chose to wait a little longer to ride in the front. There was another cluster of riders waiting for the back seat as well. That's where you feel the maximum whiplash effect. Carl insisted on the front so we could see the blood-stained tracks clearly.

Car after car filled with nervous riders and left the station. When they came back, they were laughing and relieved to be alive. Then, it was our turn. Dave and Carl took the front seat, Gabby and Roxanne right behind, and Jenny and I were behind them. A lap bar came down, pinning us firmly to the seat. There was no way a kid could stand up with this arrangement. Maybe back then, they only had seat belts? No time to ask Carl about it; we jerked out of the station and onto the open tracks.

Jenny "whoo- hooed" and grabbed my hand. What for? Aside from letting me buy stuff for her and the little touches that kept me in play, she wasn't much with me. I held her hand anyway because she was so undeniably beautiful, and any guy would be lucky to hold her hand, right? Roxanne sat right in front of Jenny, to my left, in the next car. She was hanging on tight to the handlebar in front. Gabby's hands were already in the air, along with Carl and Dave's.

282

We cruised along slowly to the base of the first climb. The cars locked into the chain drive, and we dragged upward. 'CLICK - CLICK - CLICK - CLICK' went the ratchet. The Pike fell below, and the noise of the masses faded. We climbed into the starry night with all of Long Beach glowing below. The Pacific Ocean lay peacefully to the right. A twinkle of light marked the town of Avalon way out on Catalina Island in the distance. Still, we climbed. I waved my free hand in front of my face. My hippy sister Margie said you could see trails on an acid trip. I didn't see any, I think, but all my senses were sharpened, and the dread of the first drop was building. Still, we climbed. Good God, All-Mighty, how high were we going? With no visual reference to the ground on the right and only the other track on the left, my fear of heights was kicking in. We were already a little in front of the left car. Winning the race, I guess. Finally, the track in front ran out, and we began to level out.

It was terrifying. We were at the very top of a rickety wooden erector set with nothing but death on all sides. All the nervous laughter faded away. Nobody breathed for a moment. The front car edged over the peak, and we hung there, staring straight down to darkness as the rest of the car climbed over the top. Jenny squeezed my hand hard and grabbed the handlebar with her free hand. Gabby, Carl, and Dave were forcing their hands to stay at least halfway in the air. Roxanne whimpered an F-bomb. We dropped.

The rush of speed pushed us back in our seats as the angle of descent seemed to go straight down. My stomach was in my throat, and I had to grind my torso tight to keep from throwing up. Still, we dropped. We disappeared into the tangle of tracks below and finally pulled up with triple G's pinning us down. Then it was up the next hill like a rocket. If the cars hadn't been attached to the track, I'm sure we would have shot airborne out into the ocean. But the cars were held down by the tracks, so, instead, we all went airborne against the restraint bar. How did they do this with only seatbelts holding you down? I heard someone cussing like a Navy Seabee that hit their thumb with a hammer. Then I realized it was me, and nearly everyone else. We all cussed with wild abandon laced with hysterical laughter like the Devil's Jesters. (Hey, that's a good name for a band, right?).

We shot down a ramp into a hard right turn that slammed me against Jenny and then into a cracking left that smashed her into me. Then we ran halfway up into another ratchet climb that grabbed the cars with a jerk to drag us to the top. It was a breather moment that everyone needed. The adrenaline pumped too much voltage through us with no circuit breaker. Everyone talked at once, reaffirming life and confessing secrets they didn't want to take to the grave. At least, they would have, but Carl yelled above the noise, "SECOND HILL AFTER THE CYCLONE, ON THE RIGHT!" Just as it registered what he was talking about, we went over the top and down the second drop.

This fall was not as steep or long as the first drop, but it finished with a hard banking left turn that immediately flipped right into the Cyclone. This section was a vortex of three horizontal loops, each slightly smaller in turn. With each rotation, the sensation of speed increased, and the G forces grew exponentially. Finally, on the edge of blackout, the vortex spit us out on a short straightaway with two humps for negative G's. The first one jumped us out of our seats against the restraint bar. The second one was on us in an instant... but time stood still.

We all saw the sign that warned, "DANGER - DO NOT STAND". It was old and sun-weathered, and there, on the bottom right corner of the sign, was what looked like a faded, blood-red handprint. The sign sped past as we climbed the second hump. A stabilizing spar crossed over the tracks between two pillars ahead. Too low to be safe. It was stained red in the middle. All our eyes locked on the right side of the track at the same time. We came over the hump with slightly less negative G's, and there below, a red stain extended along the track ties for about fifteen feet. I heard Roxanne say, "Oh, my God!" Then Jenny screamed.

Our eyes were on the blood-stained track. It led us into a tunnel of crisscrossing support beams. There, just inside the tunnel, barely visible in the shadows, I saw a figure of a guy wearing a '50s style Redondo High letterman's sweater. He had no head. Then we were past it in an instant. In fact, the sign, the bloodstain, and the apparition whipped by in less than two seconds. Jenny dug her nails into my arm.

Before I could scream, she let go. Our car came around a corner and pulled into the station, and stopped. The lap bar came up, and we climbed out. Everyone else who rode with us laughed, bragging about beating the other car, or just nervously chatting about the ride. I listened to hear if any of them had seen what we saw. No one said anything about it. Maybe they didn't notice because they weren't looking for it like we were. It came and went in a flash, after all. Maybe we were the only ones that could see it.

We walked out of the Cyclone structure and stool in a huddle to debrief.

Carl asked, "Did everyone see that bloody handprint on the sign?" Everyone nodded.

"And the bloodstain on the tracks?" Everyone nodded. "What did I tell you? The coaster murdered that kid right there."

Dave raised a cynical question. "How did that bloody handprint get on that sign if the accident happened down the track?"

"I don't know," defended Carl. "Maybe it splashed back or something." Dave, Gabby, and Carl started debating it while Jenny and Roxanne consoled each other. I kept waiting for someone to mention the elephant in the room, but no one did.

"Wait a minute!" I interrupted. "Hold the phone. Didn't any of you see the headless kid in the shadows?"

"Where was that?" asked Dave.

"What do you mean?" asked Carl.

"Are you kidding me?" You didn't see that headless kid in a letterman's sweater just inside the tunnel after the bloody track?"

"What are you talking about?" asked Jenny.

"I was looking at the track," said Dave.

"So was I," said Gabby.

"None of you saw it?" I couldn't believe what I was hearing. I turned to Jenny. "Then why did you scream? Why did you grab my arm?" I showed the nail marks on my forearm.

"Because," she squirmed, "you know."

"Know what?" I asked.

She answered, a bit annoyed and embarrassed. "You grabbed my leg.. right here." She touched her leg high above her knee, under her skirt, close to.. well, you know.

Gabby whistled. Dave muttered, "You dog." Roxanne cocked her head in confusion.

"I didn't grab your leg." I objected. "I was hanging on to the handlebar."

"Sure you were," said Jenny, her eyes rolling. "Don't deny it. I screamed and grabbed you because it shocked me, but it's not the first time I've been touched. That's what roller coasters are good for." She smiled coyly and gave me a little push. Roxanne looked at the ground.

"I didn't do that," I snapped, "The moment you screamed was when I saw the ghost."

Carl summed me up. "You saw a ghost that none of us saw, and Jenny got felt up by someone, but not you, even though there was no one else sitting next to her? Just own it, Lawler. You took advantage of an opportunity as any guy would. Like I certainly would." He gave Jenny a hungry look that made her bat her eyes.

The thought hit me; maybe I'm coming onto the taffy dose. I didn't have any experience with hallucinating drugs. My sister Margie told me once that they make you see what you secretly want to see. Maybe I just hallucinated that ghost to cover my sub-conscience impulse to fondle Jenny? I saw what I saw, and she says I grabbed her. How else can I explain it? But I don't think I wanted to grab Jenny; I was still dealing with Roxanne's kiss. Why would I do that? I waved my hand in front of my face. Still no trails. Maybe not that kind of drug? We walked away from the Cyclone back into the Midway. In the distance, we heard the mechanical cackle of the Pike's premier dark ride, "Laugh in the Dark". The jokes on me.

Episode 9 - Laugh in the Dark

The fact that nobody else saw that headless kid on the Cyclone was way more disturbing than if we all saw it. There was no reason to deny it if they had witnessed what I did. They all seemed to glory in what they did see; the handprint and the stains on the track. The guys are still debating it. Yet the image of that figure in an old-style lettermen's sweater is burned into my mind. (Sweater? Who does that anymore? Every high school athlete I've ever seen wears a lettermen's jacket with leather arms) It had no head, but because the others DIDN'T see it, means that IT SAW ME.

I've had this feeling before in a dream. Godzilla, King of the Monsters, comes creeping up over the hilltop with villagers scrambling to escape. He doesn't care about the villagers; he is looking straight at me. He only wants me. I run to get away, but I'm moving like I'm wading through waist-deep tar. I try to hide in a hut off to the side, but Godzilla knows I'm there, and he bends down low to look in the window, then tears the roof off and exposes me curled up in a ball. He roars, then strikes with his mouth wide open, and... that's where I wake up screaming.

We walked down the midway past the House of Mirrors. Roxanne was up in front with Gabby and Dave. I'm back with Jenny and Carl. Jenny's got my hand, and I'm walking obediently beside her, but she is laughing and jiving with Carl. Now, I'm not the sharpest knife in the drawer, but it seems plain that these two want to be together. What is she doing with me?

"Chris?" she asks, "Would you do me a favor?" (What's this? Attention?) "Here." She gave me her watch. "The clasp broke on the coaster, and I don't have any pockets. Would you carry it for me?" (So now I'm her donkey as well?) I put the watch in my pocket, and she gave me a cheap smile and turned back to Carl while still holding my hand. We walked on.

There is a curved mirror in front of the House of Mirrors that people can see themselves in as they walk past. It distorts your reflection, making you look too fat or skinny; you know the drill. We watched this gag in action before when we came this way. A lady gets distracted by the image, and a blast of air shoots up from below, blowing her skirt up like Marylyn Monroe, making everyone around laugh.

Our gang moved past, except for Jenny. She made a point of pretending she just wanted to see her reflection. She stood there for an awkwardly long time, waiting for the air blast. Finally, it blew her pleated, mid-thigh skirt up, revealing her little bikini underwear. She made no real effort to cover up as she gave everyone around a show. I know she showed me something. Her eyes were watching Carl for his reaction. The air stopped, her skirt came down, and she grabbed my hand and towed me back in place beside her. I'm in the freaking Twilight Zone.

'Laugh in the Dark' was right before us. This is it.

"Hold on, folks," said Dave. "I've got to see a man about a horse." We all looked at him, puzzled. "I've got to go pee." Nods of understanding all around. "So do I," says Gabby. "Me too," says Jenny.

Carl said, "Let's break, and get it done and meet back here in fifteen minutes. We don't want anyone peeing themselves when we see the dead guy... or if Lawler decides to grab your ass." Everyone laughed. Not funny.

The restrooms were pretty far back, near the Lido. I got my business done quick. Dave and Carl took a stall. Evidently, they had to see a man about a horse AND a wagon. See what I did there? I'm hilarious. Anyway, I was the first one back at the meeting place. Jenny was next.

We stood there for a moment, looking around.

"You know I didn't grab your leg," I said.

"Roxanne doesn't know that," she replied.

"So you are turning her against me? Why? You don't want me anyway; you want Carl."

"Maybe... we'll see. Meanwhile, I will let you know when you are dismissed."

"Why did you..." I cut it off as Gabby and Roxanne came walking up. He was enjoying the dilemma I was in, but she was looking everywhere else but at me. Carl and Dave were right behind them. We got into the line.

When we got up to the where the ride operator was seating two customers to a car, Gabby and Dave jumped in first. Carl got in the next car and yelled, "C'mon Jenny." She dropped my hand like a fish and delivered her line, "Alright, just this once," and sat beside him. That left Roxanne and me.

She got in and sat down like it was a city bus, and I sat beside her. There were no seatbelts to bother with—no time to talk, explain, or even think. The car jerked forward. We followed the others through the door into the dark, and the ride began.

Man, this ride had seen better days. It was faded, worn, smelly, and the animated ghouls' action was loose and clunky. The first thing we saw after the door closed behind us was an ugly, animated clown saying something so distorted; it could not be understood. Probably some narrative that set up the context of the ride. Even that is a step up from the typical carnival dark ride that just dragged you through meaningless displays. Someone had tried for a higher vision way back when this ride was conceived. They're dead now, and nobody cared.

I really wanted to talk to Roxanne. There was no way. Goons kept jumping out of poorly hidden blinds, axes kept falling and stopping overhead, scenes of scary clowns and demented doctors and ghoulish pirates kept coming. Music and screaming noise made relating impossible. Well, not all relating. We could both plainly see Carl and Jenny making out two cars in front as it crossed paths between blinds now and then. Aren't we supposed to be watching out for the Dead Guy? Right then, the dead guy was me.

I had been ignored, even bullied before when I was younger. Helpless anxiety was a thick, familiar fog that agreed with secret judgments I had made about myself. My old response was to wear the labels humbly, take the insults, submit to the beating, and then crawl away. Even now, if I were the only one involved here, I think I would have rolled over and shown my belly. Yet, there was Roxanne, quietly riding along, watching the mechanical scenes of suffering slide by while her hope was ground out by her best friend, who was busy tongue wrestling in the car in front. This pushed me over the edge. I started to get pissed, then angry, then furious as all the passive weakness caught fire.

Something caught my attention. There was a noise up ahead. Screaming. Not the recorded, distorted soundtrack, but real human screaming. We had entered a room with ghoulish pirates posed in scenes of revelry. I saw a commotion up ahead. I heard Gabby's voice yelling. Something was coming our way from upfront. Jenny screamed. Then the reason came into view.

It was a gory figure stumbling towards us wearing a Redondo High Seahawk football jersey. He was bloody and looked like his rotting head had been sewn back on with big ugly stitches. The ghoul moaned and cackled and was saying something about the demons of the Cyclone. It was past Gabby and Dave's car and was coming right for us.

The corpse came rushing. Roxanne couldn't find a scream. She just recoiled and braced herself with her eyes on high beam. For just a split second, the possibility that this was indeed the corpse of the dead coming at me set off a bolt of adrenaline that turned my knees to water. But, this only lasted a split second. In the second half of that second, all the pain, confusion, frustration, and injustice boiling in me geysered up. It found my fist. I leaned forward, pushing off the seat, and punched that ghoul in its face. I felt its nose crush under my knuckles, and it staggered back and knocked one of the Pirate figures across the track. The dummy got stuck under the car, and the whole ride stopped. The 'Dead Redondo Guy' got to his feet, cussing out of character, and came after me. I stepped out of the car and met him head-on. We fell into the pirate display together. This was obviously no ghost, just a guy dressed in costume and makeup. Blood was gushing from his face. He was bigger than me and got me pinned down, and was about to start working me over when he was hit from the side by a bull rush tackle. It was Gabby. They rolled to the side, and I found my feet and jumped into the melee. The lights went on, the soundtrack stopped, and a recorded voice came over the P.A. saying there were "technical difficulties, please stay seated." No one paid attention to that request. Riders left their cars and rushed to gather around the battle. Dave tried to pull the Redondo guy off, but he, in turn, was tackled by another guy. It was Carl's brother, Randy. We were all fists, kicking and grappling like An Old West Saloon fight when a gunshot went off. We froze in mid punch. The spectators dove for cover.

"What the F~~k is going on here!?" It was that big Navy man we saw getting a tattoo earlier. He was holding a smoking .45 pistol in the air.

"This kid broke my nose," said the Redondo guy. His makeup was smeared all over, and he was still bleeding.

"You came at me screaming," I said.

"I'm part of the act, you punk."

"You ain't part of the act," said the beefy sailor. "There ain't no live actors on this ride."
"It was a joke," said Carl. "A prank we were pulling on our friends. That's my brother and his friend."

About this time, two Pike security guards showed up. One of them spoke to the sailor.

"What's going on here, Mike? Who fired the shot?"

"That was me. I had to break it up before they wrecked the whole place."

"Better give me the gun. You don't want the MPs to find it on you." He took the .45 and put it in his pocket. Then he turned to all the riders crowding around. "All right folks, just follow the man with the flashlight, and he will lead you out of the ride." The people began to follow the other security guard out. "Not you folks," he said, meaning all of us involved in the fight. "You all come with me."

I was still on the ground with Gabby and the Redondo guy. Randy helped his friend up, and Sailor Mike came to help Gabby and I climb out of the mess of pirate mannequins that were jumbled all over.

"Broke his nose, huh?" said the sailor to me. "You're a pretty tough guy for your age."

"I kind of hit him before I knew it. Just impulse, I guess," I said, but inside I was saying, "Hell yeah, I'm a tough guy!" Never felt so good to be me at last. While I was getting up, I picked up a mannequin's arm that had broken off. I noticed something strange. It didn't have a metal joint to connect it to the torso. It had a broken bone sticking out. The rest was dry and stiff but obviously not plastic. "Hey, guys! Look at this."

I held it up. We all looked at the bone, then at the figure it came from. This mannequin wasn't like the others. It was dressed in a pirate outfit, but the face was caved in and ghoulish in a way that artists wouldn't think of. Here was the Dead Guy of the Pike.

"This is it. The dead kid from the Cyclone," said Dave. We looked in wonder.

"No, it's not," said Mike. "That's Old Elmer McCurdy. He's a real corpse, but he was a bank robber that got shot and killed in the thirties. My dad acquired him from a carnival wholesaler along with a bunch of other props a long time ago. We didn't know he was a real stiff. We didn't find out until his arm broke off a few years ago. I keep trying to wire it back on, but the damn thing keeps coming off."

"Is it legal to have an actual dead man's body on display?" asked Gabby.

"Maybe, Probably not," said Mike. "It's never come up since my Dad owned the ride."

"When you found out, why didn't you just bury him?" asked Roxanne.

"Why? It's good for business to have a secret. The legend of this guy brings customers. It brought all of you, didn't it?"

"We thought it was supposed to be the body of a kid from Redondo that had his head chopped off on the Cyclone Racer," said Gabby.

"Yeah, that guy," said Mike, putting McCurdy's arm down carefully next to his corpse, "We don't have that kid's body. By the time it dropped down through the tracks and got run over again, it was too mangled."

"That would have been awesome to see," said Carl. "Do you have any other dead bodies on display?"

"What the f**k, man? You hell-bent on seeing death? You think it's fun?"

"Well, we are in a funhouse, aren't we? Aren't we, 'Laughing in the Dark,' at all these ghouls?" Carl grinned at us for backup. We saw what he didn't and took a step back. Big Mike, the sailor, wasn't laughing.

"Listen, you little s**t. If you were a few years older, you might be dragging your ass through so much gore and death in the rice paddies of 'Nam you would beg for mercy. Death ain't no joke. I serve on a hospital ship off Da Nang. We get boys not much older than you who've had their arms and legs blown off, been disemboweled by shrapnel, or so badly burned, they wish they were dead. But they fight for life. And when someone does die, it's not a joke. It's a solemn ending to all their dreams and ambitions, their mother's and father's hopes, and any chance at the kind of life you kids take for granted. Even McCurdy there, was someone's little boy once. Maybe he had a girl he loved or kids that depended on him. He made bad choices and paid for it with his life. But, I bet he never thought he would be gawked at by fools like you for decades after. He has no choice; death ends all your options. Get over your love for death, kid, or it might come looking for you."

We followed Big Mile out of the ride and into a trailer that was an office. The police had been called, and they needed statements from everyone. They started with Mike. They took him to another room while we waited in the trailer.

"So who was in on it?" I asked.

"What?" asked Jenny, sitting next to Carl.

"This whole joke? Some of you had to put in some serious work to pull a prank like this off. Who is the genius?" That little bit of sarcastic flattery flushed the bird out of the bushes. Carl stood up.

"This, Ladies and Gentlemen, has been a Carl Burroughs Production." He bowed with a flourish. "I would like to thank my staff and writers, actors, and effects team for their sterling contributions to a night we will all remember." We all gave him begrudged applause. This only encouraged him. He went on.

"Credit to my co-conspirator, David West, for conceptualizing the experience and to the lovely Jennifer West, who performed her part with the acting craft of Elizabeth Taylor."

"You were in on this?" I asked Jenny. "You.. me?.. what about the drugs? What did you give me?"

Carl answered. "It's a new hardcore high from the east coast called 'Saltwater Taffy.' That was Jenny's idea. She has a talent for screwing with your mind." Jenny took a short bow.

Jenny explained, "I just wanted to give you something to think about. It was fun, right?"

Right. Fun. I turned to Gabby.

"Don't tell me you were in on it. Am I the only sucker here?"

"I prefer the term, 'Audience' but no, I wasn't in on it, but I smelled a rat. I knew something was going on. I just sat back and enjoyed the ride." He slapped five with Carl, appreciating his craft.

"What about you?" I asked Roxanne. "Did you know?"

"I didn't know anything. I didn't even want to come, remember?"

"That's right. You were for real all night long." I sat down and thought about that. She tossed me a questioning look. Was I for real?

Dave said, "Let's not forget Carl's brother, Randy," (who gave a salute without looking up). "None of this could have happened without him and his friend.. what's your name?"

The guy was sitting there still wearing the blood-stained Redondo jersey, holding an ice pack to his nose. He mumbled something that sounded like, "Boof Wimiss."

"Well," said Randy, "Bruce not the best actor or stuntman. He did ok until Lawler broke his nose."

"I'm sorry about that, man. You were just trying to pull a prank, and I respect that."

He looked at me through one eye and grunted acceptance.

"One question, how did you get from the Cyclone to the Laugh in the Dark and change costume and makeup so fast?"

Bruce looked at me for a second. "I wasn't on the Cyclone."

"Right after the camelbacks, where you put the fake bloodstain on the tracks? That wasn't you?"

"I was here with Randy, getting ready for you punks. What are you talking about?"

I didn't answer, but a chill ran up my spine. Someone came and took poor Bruce Billus, or Woomis, whatever his name was, to a first-aid trailer, and we didn't see him again. Not for years. Then he hit the big screen and we all saw him. You know what? He got better.

Sailor Mike came back and told us he had smoothed everything out with the police, and they didn't need our statements after all. I think he didn't want to take a chance that we would spill the beans about dead man McCurdy. We just had to sign a release to avoid being charged with destroying Pike property. After signing, we were kicked out of the office and expelled from the Pike.

"I'm surprised that they didn't call our parents after all this," said Roxanne.

"This is Long Beach," said Randy. "They don't rat you out to your Mommy and Daddy every time you stir up a little trouble. I'm going to get my truck. Wait here."

The ride back to Redondo was not as fun as the ride out. I was still wearing my shorts and paisley shirt I put on in the morning. It had been a reasonably warm day, but now I was freezing in the back of Randy's pick up. We were all cold. Jenny openly snuggled up to Carl, now that the play-acting was over. Dave and Gabby had called dibs right off and were in the cab. (So much for chivalry). I looked at Roxanne. She was shivering. I slipped up next to her and put an arm around her. She folded herself within and laid her head on my shoulder. Her warmth poured into me. We listened to the muffled sound of Roy Orbison coming from inside the cab. 'Only the Lonely.'

We didn't talk much all the way back. Randy dropped us off at Dave and Jenny's house. He left with Carl to go home. We went inside and called our parents for a pickup. Mr. and Mrs. West were already in bed, so no cookies and hot chocolate to greet us. Jenny 'invited' us to sit outside on her porch to wait for pick up. Before she closed the door, she remembered something.

"You have my watch," she said and stuck out her hand.

I reached in my pocket and pulled it out, and put it in her palm. A piece of folded cardboard was with it. She opened it and read aloud, "No."

"What's this?" she asked.

"That's for you," I said. She didn't get it. She just dropped it with a 'whatever' and closed the door.

Gabby's dad was the first to arrive. Gabby got in the car and left with a "Later" tossed at me.

That gave Roxanne and me a few moments alone. If I were a few years older, I might have known what to do with it. All I could come up with was, "You want to hang out sometime?"

"Sure." She picked up my little note that Jenny had dropped and wrote her phone number on the other side. "I know a bookstore in Hermosa where they let you browse while they play whole Frank Zappa albums. We should meet up there sometime."

Just then, her dad drove up.

"Thanks for being with me, Chris. You're a cool guy." She gave me a 'dad safe' little kiss and walked away tossing, "call me" over her shoulder. Then she was gone. I sat on the bench and thought about life.

When my dad, El Jack, showed up in his van, I expected the worst. I got in, and we drove for a little in silence.

"You put your Mom through the wringer tonight. Your little sister cried her eyes out. We didn't know if you were dead or alive. What gave you the idea you could drop out of sight without a word?"

Time to play my get-out-of-jail card. "You did. I asked you in your office earlier today, remember? You said yes." He knew I had him.

"Pretty tricky play, boy. You got one by me." He looked at me with new respect. Maybe I wasn't such a choir boy after all. "Fair enough. Tell me about it."

I told him all about the Pike, the Cyclone, Jenny and Roxanne (that raised his eyebrows), and the fight in the dark ride. He ate up every word. By the time we got home, he was tussling my hair and laughing like a pirate with me. He pass blocked my Mom from tackling me and let me get to bed. Syndie got in bed with me and went to sleep at my feet like a puppy. Before I could drop off, Margie cracked my door and whispered a question into the dark.

"See your girl?"

"Two girls. They were fighting over me."

"Are you a bad-ass now?"

"I don't know, maybe, halfway."

"Which half, the bad or the ass?"

"I'll tell you what happened tomorrow. Then you can tell me."

"Just one more question. Did you play your 'No'?"

"Sort of."
"Then you are sort of a bad-ass. See you in the morning."

She closed the door. I drifted off to sleep thinking about that Spooky kind of girl who likes Frank Zappa. And me.

~ ~ ~

The End

Epilogue

Dave West -became a writer after college and pens a column for the Daily Breeze.

Jenny West -became a cheerleader at Redondo, got pregnant, and had to drop out halfway through her senior year. Not sure who the father is.

Randy -went on to join a heavy metal band as a lead singer. They made a little noise, sold a few albums, then broke up over girl trouble. Now he works at a liquor store in Five Corners, Hermosa.

Carl -became a star in the theatre department and played football for the Seahawks. I ran into him only once, three years later across the line from me on the football field. Dave was a defensive lineman, and I was an offensive guard for the Mira Costa Mustangs. I got to knock his block off all day. I owned him.

Gabby -stayed my best friend through our teenage years. He joined the Air Force after high school at traveled the world. He's still out there in some hidden corner of the world, living large and taking names.

Roxanne -and I became great friends and shared a love for nerd science, monster movies, and Frank Zappa. We started to tease romance but realized we were not cast for that role. There was still too much fun left in our childhood to drag along a heavy heartbreak. I always had her back, and she had mine. She went to

Bishop Montgomery HS for the science program. After graduating from Cal Tech, she became a scientist working for TRW. She married an astronaut. I was in her wedding. I couldn't be the best man, so she made me the Maid of Honor. I know, right?

Chris Lawler -grew up a genuine son of the South Bay. Mira Costa High School got hold of me and shaped me into the young man who stepped into adulthood with some trepidation. In particular, Bill Cooper and the coaching staff for Mustang football gave me the crucible I so sorely needed to refine manhood.

The Pike -got soo seedy, they tore it down and build a retail zone on the site that is still called the Pike. They incorporated a decorative roller coaster motif you can still see today, but it's not where the original Cyclone Racer was. That spot now has a restaurant on it. Rumor is, it's haunted.

Dead Man McCurdy -was discovered by a prop man working on location while they shot an episode of the Six Million Dollar Man. He was as crumbly as a cracker. You can Google all about it. Everyone was surprised except an old sailor named Mike and maybe a few others. They buried him at last. Rest In Pieces.

~Finis~

Thank you for taking this ride with me. It's been an education writing like this. I hope you have enjoyed it. In A Son of the South Bay, Part II, I will drag you through my endless days of a teenager at Mira Costa high school. Then I'll take you with me to tour the strange adventures that happened to me as a young man ready to dive into life. Until then...

...God bless the South Bay and the Tribe that grew there. I love you all. Blessings.

Acknowledgments

I want to thank all my South Bay tribe dispersed around the world who shared this special beach town paradise. We reconnected on several Facebook Groups and you gave me a home to plant this little garden of memories. Your love and enthusiasm for my writings watered this garden and created the jungle of stories you hold in your hands.

Special thank you to Lonnie Baker Bradley, a surfer girl and a gifted writer who found me, mentored me and encouraged me to give this gift.

This book would not be in your hands if it weren't for my best friend, Gerald (Gabby) Hayes. Yea, *that* Gabby. Writing professionally is his wheel-house, not mine. He produced this book and helped bring it to market. Check out his own book of short stories, *The Rats of Plainville: Tales from the Heartland,* also available on Amazon.

About the Author

It's strange to write about myself in the third person but not as strange as the experience of holding a book in my hands (or his hands?) that Chris Lawler wrote in the decrepit years of his old age when he should already be dead and rotting. I guess there is a God after all, right? So, who is Chris Lawler? He is mainly a semi-retired furniture repairman, a serial social media poster and the (alleged) sire of three kids who keep calling him father even though they never saw nothing and can't prove anything. He has been married to Susan Lawler for nearly forty years (the best twenty five years of her life, she claims). They have lived in Whittier California, in the same house, since the first day they were married and still thought it was a good idea. Even though he's lived way over there on the other side of L.A. from his beloved Beach Towns, he brazenly claims ALL the sun kissed sandy beaches of Southern California as his back yard. What an arrogant jerk, right?

Made in the USA
Las Vegas, NV
24 December 2020